MW01600763

WHAT PEOPLE ARE SAYING ABOUT
LIFE AFTER UNSHACKLED

Gene's life is a story of faith, forgiveness, redemption, and hope. *Life After Unshackled* shows the power of what God can do in a person's life.

Chad Hennings
Founder, Wingmen Ministries
3x Super Bowl Champion

After encountering Jesus in prison, Gene McGuire emerged from a 35-year sentence for a crime he himself did not commit with a passion to share his testimony of God's faithfulness—on television, in high schools, restaurants, and prisons. In this book, Gene invites us on his journey through life, post-incarceration. From the people he has met along the way, the challenges he has faced, and the providential opportunities he has experienced, Gene's story is one that reminds us that God's grace never leaves us the same, and in his own closing words, *"life after you've found yourself in His story is truly worth living."* Read this and you will be inspired.

Adam C. Wright, Ph.D.
President, Dallas Baptist University

Gene has lived a life most of us know nothing about. Rather than embracing bitterness and being a victim of tragic circumstances, he chooses to inspire and motivate others through his story. I encourage you to learn more about his life and the miracles he has experienced. In doing so, you will no doubt find encouragement and a greater ability to see God's blessings in your own life. I highly recommend this book.

Dan Dean
Lead Singer of Phillips, Craig, and Dean
Legacy Pastor, Heartland Church, Carrollton, TX

I

Gene McGuire has one of the most memorable testimonies I've ever heard. What impacts me most is the way he shares his story without even the slightest indication of bitterness. It is so amazing to witness someone who has had every reason to give up on life and faith literally allow God to build a life of purpose from the ashes of past injustice. This book picks up where *Unshackled* left off and takes you on a journey from freedom to purpose and uncommon favor. Gene's life is not only an inspiration, it is also a blueprint for anyone who has been handed a difficult past and has decided to choose true freedom in Christ.

Michael Bethany
Worship Pastor, Gateway Church, Southlake, TX

On the pages of this new incredible book, my friend Gene McGuire's willingness to be transparent and vulnerable makes the truth he is relaying easy to digest. If you're tired of circling around the same struggles, you will find an accessible off-ramp to a freer and fuller life in *Life After Unshackled*. Don't count yourself out just yet; your challenges are only the starting place of God's purpose in your life.

Steve Abraham
Pastor, New Life Community Church, Oxnard, CA

"What? Are you serious?" This was my response as my Father eagerly told me he had met the man who should become our second company chaplain. He told me his name was Gene McGuire and that he had been released from prison after nearly 35 years, having been sentenced to life. My fear and trepidation washed away once I met Gene and heard his story. In the years since, I've remained amazed at how contagious Gene's joy for life and thankfulness in everything is to us all. In *Life After Unshackled*, Gene brings us with him as he walks in faith and youthful zeal into his new life of freedom!

Joel Vinyard
Owner & President, Babe's Chicken Dinner House, Bubba's Cooks Country and Sweetie Pie's Ribeyes

Gene's passion for Christ and love for life and those around him is evident when you meet him. After hearing his story and reading it in both *Unshackled* and *Life After* what is so incredible is his positive outlook, spirit of forgiveness and sheer determination to maximize his impact for The Kingdom with the time God has given him regardless of the circumstances. Gene's story is impactful for all of us, regardless of age or station in life. Gene gives us a great example of how to be thankful in all things (1 Thessalonians 5:18). I am honored to a very small part of his very big story.

Howard W. Harris, MD
Texas Orthopedic Specialists, PLLC

This is one of the most enjoyable books I have ever read. Gene's book combines a great redemption story with the follow through chapters of his radically changed life which have proven successful when measured by an eternal yardstick. Gene weaves in entertaining stories and encouraging challenges to his readers while always pointing to Scripture and teaching readers the real meaning of success, priorities and forgiveness. *Life After Unshackled* gives us a glimpse at what 34 years, 9 months and 15 days looks like in molding the heart of a man who is willing to surrender. This book will encourage you to live better. It did me.

Scott Fish
Founder & CEO, Tri-Win Direct

Gene McGuire can be described in many ways: friend, man of God, disciplined, focused, lovable servant, and more. My favorite is Dad.

It was Gene's heart to serve others that was amazing to me. I saw him serve when few others would. His servant's heart allowed him to approach others and speak to them. Gene is a people person. He is an investor in people. His greatest dividends are realized in the growth of the lives he has touched.

I am no exception. Gene's service, love and kindness have impacted my life for several years, both in and outside of prison. One of the lessons he has taught me—and one that remains with me is "always remain teachable, correctable and moldable; no one likes a know-it-all." It sounds simple, I know, but implementing this into my life has been anything but. Another lesson he engrained in me is "relationships are always more important than the project." No matter how important a task or project is, don't ever jeopardize a relationship for it.

Gene is ultimately about relationships. Just like anything in this lifetime that is worthwhile, we need to cultivate and manage our relationships. Fruitful relationships don't just happen, they are intentional. Jesus was an amazing relationship builder. He went out of his way to meet people where they were. But he was never content to leave them there. Gene replicates Jesus in this way. I've learned so much from Gene. He disciplined me, encouraged me, discipled me, but most of all, he's always loved me. To this day, I consider him a father figure in my life.

Since his release from prison, Gene has not stopped serving, loving and being available to others. His desire to see others grow, to know the Lord loves them and to become fruitful in their faith drives him every day.

Life After Unshackled will impact your perspective, allowing you to see that no obstacle is too big, and no failure so devastating that it cannot be redeemed, restored and renewed.

Orlando Colon
Union Organizer, Local 202, Philadelphia, PA

I met Gene several years ago through a mutual friend. Gene spoke to our men's group at church. I was immediately drawn to his powerful story, and the authentic nature of his testimony. But what was even more incredible to me is how full of joy this man is! I have had Gene speak to my employees twice over the past six years and he has been a hit each time. You cannot help but love Gene, because the Spirit of God is so palpable in his life. I am so glad he has decided to write a new book chronicling all the things that God is has been doing through him since he wrote Unshackled. I highly recommend you read his new book *Life After Unshackled* to learn more about the power of God in a man who has been freed to be His witness to the world.

Bob Baldridge
CEO, Varispark

If the devil thought Gene McGuire's testimony was finished the moment he walked out of prison a free man on April 3, 2012, he was dead wrong. He couldn't have been more wrong. I don't know of too many men who have a testimony as gripping as Gene's. After all, how many men have served 35 years of a life-sentence for a crime they didn't commit?

Gene's testimony since getting out of prison is as great if not greater than before. But the story line has changed from "look what God has done," to "look what God is doing."

I have actively ministered to incarcerated men for most of my life. I've learned that it is actually easier for them to live for the Lord while they are incarcerated than when they are released. Gene's story continues to be one of discipleship and obedience, but not without temptations and trials. The stories continue to be riveting, but now include a multitude of people who have been transformed through Gene's testimony.

As a reader, you will now be part of Gene's "greater" testimony.

Larry Titus
President, Kingdom Global Ministry

In the Spring of 2018, a friend at my church told me about a guy I had to meet and gave me a copy of *Unshackled: From Ruin to Redemption*, the Gene McGuire Story. I read the book in a couple of days; I couldn't put it down, reading late into the night. I've recommended Unshackled, now, to so many people, and was so excited about Gene's story of redemption that I invited him to speak at our church on July 1, 2018. God used Gene in a powerful way at Grace Fellowship as he shared his story with humility and authenticity. I now count him as a friend and I am very excited about his new book, *Life After Unshackled*. I believe God is going to use it to encourage and transform the lives of many people.

B.J. Rutledge
Legacy Pastor, Grace Fellowship Church, Paradise, Texas

I have enjoyed getting to know Gene through my time at Babes Chicken in Frisco. Having read his story in *Unshackled*, and now reading *Life After Unshackled*, learning about the blessings and the struggles of life after being incarcerated have been eye-opening. Seeing how God brought new life out of a life sentence inspires hope. It is truly amazing how God opens doors ... and blesses those who walk through them.

Gabe Higgins
Server, Babe's Chicken Dinner House, Frisco, TX

LIFE
AFTER UNSHACKLED

Gene

By

GENE MᶜGUIRE

With Darin Michael Shaw

Published by:
Gene McGuire Ministries
PO Box 163443
Fort Worth Texas 76161
www.genemcguire.org

21 20 19 18 17 10 9 8 7 6 5 4 3 2 1

Library of Congress Cataloging-in-Publication Data
McGuire, Eugene

ISBN: 978-1-7320126-3-9 (Hardcover)

BISAC Category:
REL012040 RELIGION / Christian Life / Inspirational
REL024000 BIOGRAPHY & AUTOBIOGRAPHY / Criminals & Outlaws

FOREWORD

Gene began the closing chapter of his first book, *Unshackled*, with these words: *"I received a life sentence, and along the way, I found life."* He closed that part of his story with an invitation and a promise: *"Turn to Jesus. Cling to Jesus. The best is yet to come!"*

In *Life After Unshackled,* Gene offers us the rest of the story, or at least the *next part* of the story. Picking up right where he'd left off, with his release from prison on April 3, 2012, Gene walks us forward through a series of rather unique *life-after-incarceration* experiences, sometimes prompting laughter and at other times, tears. Like he did with *Unshackled*, Gene's storytelling in *Life After* keeps us engaged and turning pages . . . to see what door God opens next.

I have heard Gene share his testimony several times and I've never made it through with dry eyes. No matter who you are, or where you are on life's journey, Gene's unassuming, casual, friendly manner puts you at ease. And his heart comes through, speaking to your heart.

God gave me a chicken business in order to encourage and raise up young people to the point that they will see Jesus Christ in who we are and the way we conduct our business. It is a particular blessing to me when some of these kids come back years later, all grown up, and let us know that something they heard or some experience they had here inspired them. We have some 1,700 employees, give or take. We added Gene as a chaplain to our employees in July of 2013. His ministry here has encompassed everything from being a smiling face and a listening ear to officiating weddings and funerals; from praying with a teenager about their struggles at school to holding a bedside vigil with a parent who had just been told their child will not recover from injuries . . . facing the anguishing decision to turn off life support. God has gifted Gene with a Christ-like heart for people.

Gene has single-handedly changed my perception of incarceration. His very direct view into prison life and culture has been a great education for me. More than I'd anticipated, we have a number of employees who have an incarcerated loved-one. They are anxious to get true answers to their questions. They appreciate that Gene gets what they and their loved ones are going through. But the life-applicable lessons of Gene's story don't stop there. Lessons of rubber-meets-the-road faith—in waiting on and trusting in God; in bearing with, loving and forgiving others; in finding hope for the future and healing for the past; in holding onto truth and letting go of folly—we've all been there, and Gene's story relates.

God's promise to us is that, *in all things*, His grace is sufficient. This is why I'm excited this new book is in your hands: Gene's testimony is living proof. And I know his story will touch you. For as Gene says in the close of this second book, *"while each of us and our stories are unique, we find ourselves together in one, overarching story—His story."* In each of our lives, His story continues to unfold.

Paul Vinyard

Owner, Babe's Chicken Dinner House, Bubba's Cooks County, Sweetie Pie's Ribeyes

ACKNOWLEDGMENTS

Grateful is how I feel towards Darin Michael Shaw, my collaborative writer, for the trusted friendship and work relationship that has developed over the course of six years, two books and numerous weekends spent together. It was indeed his voice over numerous phone calls saying, "When do you want to write that second book and update all your readers of *Unshackled*?" His voice would in time be echoed by dozens of servers at Babe's Chicken asking the same question. Darin provided the motivation for me to begin writing the book you're holding, *LIFE After Unshackled*.

I may have met Richard Harmer six years ago through an agency we initially hired to build a website and platform for the first book *Unshackled*, yet God intended a friendship for life. Richard and his wife Lori have invited me to every family celebration since that day. They are extraordinary people. Whether the occasion was a birthday along the Llano River in Castell, TX or gathering around their pool in stars and stripes shorts to celebrate the 4th of July or wearing matching red and black plaid flannel pajamas around the family Christmas Tree, with Brooklyn and Canaan celebrating the Savior, I have been so blessed to be part of it all.

How could I not mention my brothers Warner Batty, aka Big Moses, Scott Dougherty, Shots Boyd, Jose Cruz and Will "Surf" Hull? These men are serving life sentences, and their friendship inspires me to live radically serving the Lord Jesus Christ. Our friendships have continued over four decades and while my location has changed, they remain my closest friends and most enthusiastic supporters. They bring so much joy and pride to my life by overcoming many struggles by the blood of the Lamb and the word of their testimony. I sure appreciate you men!

Many who have read *Unshackled, From Ruin to Redemption* have responded with heart-felt words. If that is you, thank you so much! Your support is amazing. Hearing your personal testimonies of reconciliation to the Lord and how you received fresh hope to move forward through difficult circumstances strengthens my soul. Your miraculous, redemptive story have brought tears to my eyes and caused numerous fist pumps with shouts of hallelujah as I've read your words.

Larry Titus, your profound insights and applications from the Bible have long mentored me. I recall your biblical charge: In the presence of God and of Jesus Christ, who will judge the living and the dead, and in view of His appearing and His kingdom, I give you this charge: Preach the word; Be prepared in season and out of season; correct, rebuke, encourage-with great patience and careful instruction (2 Timothy 4:1-2 NIV).

Paul Vinyard, I truly believe you acted in faith on a guy you met for the first time and saw more purpose through the eyes of Christ in the kingdom of God than he did at that divine moment in time. Your decision to hire a chaplain trained behind barbed wire fences and locked prison gates is a sign of your empathy and sage experience. Your compassion towards your employees in how you view their needs, is a rare find in the marketplace and is what I have experienced from you since the day we met. Thank you for pursuing, trusting and hiring me. Thank you for the opportunity to partner with you and entire family to help raise up godly leaders throughout Babe's, Sweetie Pie's Ribeyes and Bubbas.

Thanks also to all the supervisors who I have the pleasure to work with: Kristin, Uncle Joe, Bill, Ed, Jay and Andy.

Thank you to all the general managers: Debra, Eliacim, Ryan, Bryan, Walter, Chris, Tim, Yvo, Mark, Joe, Jason, Scott, Patrick, John, Rick, and AJ. Y'all facilitate and help us reach many with the Gospel of Jesus Christ.

TABLE OF CONTENTS

PREFACE

[SCI Phoenix, November 12, 2019] *Good morning, Men. This will be one of the greatest days of your lives. Today, if you choose, your life and your heart will be forever changed.*

You have the privilege to meet one of your own today—a man who was sentenced to Life without the possibility of parole for a murder he didn't commit. He was shocked when, at 17 years of age, he heard the judge say, "... for the rest of your natural life."

He served 34 years, nine months and 15 days ... and was miraculously released. He will tell you more.

I'm here today to introduce this man to you. He and I have a lot in common. I also spent time in prison ... every weekend for the 25 years that I visited him. That's the better way to experience this place, as a visitor rather than an inmate. Each weekend I'd come in, and this man and I spent time together, talking about our lives and talking about our faith.

I know this man. I know his heart. I know his soul. He is the real deal. Over 25 years of visits, calls, letters and attending special functions at the prison—even seeing him in his cell, a poignant moment for us both, as he will tell you—I've come to know him as a man of genuine and authentic faith. I've observed as he's lived a life of love and service to those in prison and beyond. Most miraculously—I've sensed in him no bitterness or anger for what he's been through, but rather gratefulness and thanksgiving.

Whether incarcerated or not, many of us live our lives imprisoned, trapped behind bars of anger, resentment, rebellion, lust or unforgiveness. If any of that sounds familiar, and should you choose to listen to this man—allow his story to speak into yours—I promise you, you'll be better for it.

I'm proud to be here with you today, and to introduce a man I love and admire, a man I am so proud to call my Main Man in Christ, and my dear friend, Gene McGuire.

I've had the privilege of having Rob introduce me many times and in many different settings. This day seemed extra special. Maybe because of where we were, at SCI Phoenix, back inside the Pennsylvania prison system. Or maybe it's because of who else was there: my friend Will, aka "Surf," was finishing his sentence up at Phoenix. And my dear friend Patty had come with us that morning. This was Patty's first time seeing me share my testimony in a prison setting. But this wasn't the first time she'd heard Rob introduce me.

. . .

A few months after my release from prison, after I'd already relocated to Texas, I flew back to Pennsylvania for a couple of speaking engagements and stayed with Rob. During my visit, Rob and a girl he was dating contrived a double date; *just so happened that Rob's girlfriend had a single friend* ... everyone is a matchmaker.

Rob, however, takes particular joy in this. He will tell you himself, he can't wait to see people's reactions to me. He teases me all the time. We'll be driving, and he'll say, "I'm going to roll through this stop sign so the cops stop us, and I'll tell them, 'Officer, you might want to run this guy's ID!'"

The evening of the double date, we all sat down at Bonefish Grill. I'll be honest and tell you, first impression—Patty is a beautiful lady. The usual conversation unfolded. She told me a little about her life and career. She was divorced, and not seeing anyone at the moment. "I dated a cop for a while," she said.

Rob kicked me under the table and teased, "I wonder if he knows you, Gene."

Then it was my turn. Patty asked, "What do you do?"

I had moved down to Texas, you'll remember, to work with my friend and mentor Larry Titus' Kingdom Global Ministry. At this point in time, I'd just left KGM and started working for my friend James' roofing business. I rolled all that into my answer—a few months of ministry followed by a few months of roofing.

"What did you do before that?" she asked.

Rob's grin grew ear to ear. "*Yes!* What *did* you do before that, Gene?"

"I was away," I said.

Assuming I meant that I was traveling or something, Patty asked, "Oh? Where were you?"

"I was incarcerated."

You really had to be there; Rob's grin went full-on Cheshire Cat, and Patty's face went a little pale. "Oh," she said, reaching for her glass to take a sip of wine.

A little backstory here: Patty has a bunch of police officers in her family, and she'd dated cops. You could see her wheels turning. "What were you in prison for?"

"Homicide," I said. Patty took another sip of wine. I'm thinking this is an absolute disaster. Rob is thinking this couldn't be going any better!

"I suppose you're going to tell me you didn't do it," Patty joked.

I delivered the punchline: "That's right. I didn't do it."

At this, Patty gave a nervous laugh and said, "I think I need a cigarette." Although I don't smoke, I asked her if I could accompany her outside. We talked more. I gave her a little more of the story. We hit it off and decided we'd see one another again.

Patty tells the story of a family get-together not long after we'd met. One of her relatives asked, "Are you seeing anyone?"

Taking a page out of Rob's playbook, she relished the moment: "As a matter of fact, I met this guy who was in prison ..."

Her relatives were like, "And you ran the other way, right?"

"No," Patty told them, "I invited him over and cooked him dinner."

Patty and I dated for almost a year. In the end, we both realized that her life is based in Pennsylvania and mine in Texas—we were just at different stations in life. But I love Patty with all my heart. She is one of my dearest friends.

———

Two hundred men packed into the auditorium that day at SCI Phoenix. The chapel team there led us in about 20 minutes of worship. Guys shouted 'Hallelujah!' and 'Praise the Lord!' Anticipation was building throughout the room, and excitement welled up in me. You could have heard a pin drop as Rob introduced me.

When he got to the end, "my dear friend, Gene McGuire ..." the men rose to their feet and applauded. It was a very warm welcome.

As I stood before these men, looking into their eyes, a feeling of hope began to permeate the room. If God had *unshackled* me, He is able to set them free, too. This was my opportunity to speak with them about the life God has for each of them ...

And for *you*, as you read this book, *Life After Unshackled*.

CHAPTER 1

RIGHT THERE

"Right there." Orlando nodded his head to the left. "See that corner? That's where my crime happened."

I could hear the regret in his voice and see it in his expression. He even avoided looking over himself. Instead, he focused on the traffic light, anxious for it to change and allow us to roll away.

A warm, early Fall day, a busy South Philly corner. People were coming and going—some looking to cross the street, others waiting for a bus. Life moves on. As if nobody knows—

A young man lost his life right where they're standing. Family and friends lost a loved one. Another young man—a neighborhood boy of 17—was sent to prison for 24-48 years. Tragedy all around, because of something that happened *right there*, in that very spot.

The car was quiet for a few blocks. I imagined the scene, recalling what Orlando had shared with me years earlier—he'd walked up to the victim's car, shouted "Hand over the money!" He presented a gun ... *BOOM!*

I broke the silence: "Is it difficult for you to drive by that corner?"

"No," he said. I watched Orlando as he drove on. He was expressionless. He'd gone someplace else in his mind—thinking, processing.

I know the feeling.

Three years earlier, I'd walked back into the Marine Room Tavern where my crime occurred in June of 1977. It had been nearly 40 years. It felt like sacred ground, like *I'm not worthy to be here*. It is the site of my deepest and most abiding regret. I can't go back and undo it, can't fix it.

Conversation picked up again as we neared our destination. Orlando was taking Henry and me to meet his childhood friend Jik. He'd given Jik a copy of *Unshackled* a few months earlier. Orlando said, "Jik really wants to meet you." But the honor was going to be all mine—Jik the Barber is pretty much a North Philly legend. Look him up.

Best friends since kindergarten, Orlando filled us in on Jik's story. He was on his way to a very successful life as a barber until drugs unraveled it all. Somewhere in the freefall, Jik was arrested and on his way to jail when he escaped from the back of a police transport van. That's an impressive feat—and lends to the legend—but it's what happened after they caught him that begins Jik's *real* story.

An escape risk, they locked Jik in solitary confinement and told him to get used to it. An 8x8 room. Walls. No one. Nothing. Jik cried out in prayer, "Lord, if You'll get me out of this solitary confinement, I'll follow You." And Jik is a man of his word.

Climbing a narrow set of stairs, I realized just how limited space is in this part of town. If Orlando weren't leading the way, I don't think I'd have found this place. Top of the stairs, the door opened and there he was, this fly, edgy-looking guy—thin beard, arms sleeved in tattoos, baseball cap on backwards. When he saw us, that edgy look instantly melted into the most warm and welcoming smile and greetings. You know how it feels when someone is genuinely glad to see you? *That*.

He had a customer, mid-cut, when we walked in. We all talked and laughed while Jik did his thing. A no-frills space, a single black leather barber chair … and a skilled craftsman. As I watched Jik with trimmer and comb in hand, a verse from Proverbs came to my mind: "Do you see a man skillful in his work?

He will stand before kings; he will not stand before obscure men" (22:29).

Our conversation and laughter centered on where the Lord placed each of us. It is unbelievable, really. Each of our characters had been changed by the grace of God. We needed to be changed radically before He could use us radically. We all recognized He had set us free in order to display His mercy and grace. There's Henry, working as an electrician and counseling drug addicts. Orlando, moving up the ladder in the local labor union in Philly. Me, a chaplain ministering to the employees and guests of a chain of Christian-owned restaurants in Texas. God changed our identities and our destinies when we accepted Christ as Savior.

My mind flashed back some 30 years. I wrote about it in *Unshackled*—a brief window when I had an older cellie named Clyde. Seeing him climb the stairs on the range, stop half-way to lean on the rail and catch his breath—his life was labor. And old-man Kenny. A sweet old man, he'd been in so long everybody liked him—he was like everyone's grandpa. Hunched over, hobbled, short of breath. I hated the thought of aging and declining health behind bars like these guys; hated the thought that, one day, *that* would be me. I would pray: *Lord, I don't want to live in a geriatric unit with other prisoners having to feed me and bathe me. I don't want to die in here.*

But we are no longer destined to grow old and die in a prison hospital like some of the close friends we'd made. It's surreal. *Here we are today*, hanging out in Jik's Barber Shop! In Philadelphia! I'm sharing and laughing with guys I'd spent the better part of three decades with in prison. God is so good!

Once the guy in the chair was done, Henry jumped up and shouted, "I'm next!" Jik went to work on Henry's high and tight.

These guys, the sound of clippers, the smell of aftershave and the banter—it all took me back to barber shop experiences in prison, and guys getting their regular two-month cuts. All similarity ended there, though. Because Jik is skilled. He'd developed his talents as a youngster, cutting hair on the streets of Philly. Prison barbers are hit or miss. A lot more miss than hit. You sit in some newbie's chair and ... *Good luck, brother!* I remember a lot of guys getting out of the chair furious. After my first bad cut, I was more than willing to pay the more skilled barber a couple packs of cigarettes to sit in his chair instead.

As we shared about God's grace, how He'd changed each of our lives, His goodness overwhelmed us. Henry summed up what we were all feeling: "If Jesus hadn't interrupted my life years ago, I wouldn't be here today."

Jik's next appointment walked in. He had to get back to work. We took a quick picture together and said our good-byes.

Once downstairs, Henry took the lead through Center City, leading us into a South Philly neighborhood. He had us turning left, then right; he was like a human GPS. Sometimes down a block, sometimes through an alley; concrete stoops, doorways and awnings lined the sidewalks. His head down, Notre Dame Fighting Irish ball cap spun backwards, Henry walked with purpose. I can't remember if it was me or Orlando, but one of us finally asked: "Where are we going?"

"Gotta show you something," Henry said.

Every once in a while, I have these odd recollections. Like déjà vu, you know? That powerful feeling like you've been here before. Now, with me and Orlando falling in behind Henry, I recalled how they line you up to go anywhere and everywhere in prison. I can't tell you how many times I'd had this very experience; the three of us, and other guys, walking in a line. But this time, we weren't in prison. We were three free men, walking down city streets. What a great moment. *Thank you, Lord.*

We walked for a while, Orlando and I were teasing and having fun. Then suddenly we stopped. The feel of things changed instantly. Eyes averted to the ground and his hands pushing deep into his pockets, Henry spoke up: "I was sitting over there on that stoop, drinking a Mountain Dew and doing whippets. These three kids came up, like they were going to pass me by. But one of them spun around and sucker-punched me. Then they all overpowered me, stole my money and my gold chain ... they took my whippets and my bike."

I looked around, imagining the scene as a 17-year-old Henry had experienced it. "This is where it all started," he said. Being here was emotional for him. We stood still for a few moments, taking it all in. Once Henry regained his composure, he said, "Come on," and we were walking again.

I wondered, *What's a whippet?* I'd have to wait for an answer.

"I staggered out of this alley," he pointed. "My eye was cut and bleeding pretty good. Right over there, a few of my old heads—corner boys—saw that I was all messed up. They wanted to know what happened. Everybody got all fired up, and, next thing I knew, we were off to find the guys who did it."

We walked on. Years ago, I'd read a transcript of Henry's testimony. I knew where this story was going. And where we were heading. "Up here," he said, "we saw three guys and they had whippets in their hands. The corner boys were like, 'These are the guys!'"

We stopped again, in the middle of the sidewalk on South Street. Henry put his hands back in his pockets and looked down. I knew. The pained look on his face confirmed—

"Right here," he said, "I stabbed the guy. He fell right there," pointing directly down between our feet. We stood in the very spot where, some 40 years earlier, one young man tragically died ... and where another's fate was sealed— *life without the possibility of parole.* "We took off running," he continued. "It wasn't long before I heard the news reports; heard that the guy died. I knew it was serious. I turned myself in at the police station and was charged with homicide."

I was in the courtroom in 2016 at Henry's re-sentencing. I'll never forget the emotional plea from the victim's brother, or how Henry turned his entire body, out of respect, to look the man in the eye as he spoke. My heart was in my throat. You could've heard a pin drop in those moments. I think everyone in the courtroom held their breath like I did, anxious for what the man would say.

He began by expressing the great loss he'd felt, growing up without his brother, and the pain it caused his entire family. Without diminishing the crime or the punishment, he expressed his confidence in Henry, whose genuine remorse was evident in the way he'd committed his life to serving others. *The victim's brother asked the judge for Henry's release.* Things would never be the same. You can't go back. You can't undo what's done. But to see glimpses of forgiveness, healing and redemption—*life after*—is really something.

What we shared this day was very special to me. Three guys—who were all teenagers at the time of our crimes—remembering how it had all happened, so fast. In an instant, lives were lost. And other lives were forever altered. Now, here we were: friends having spent decades together in prison back together on what felt like a memorial walk, revisiting and remembering—and realizing the depth and power of God's redemptive love.

"What the heck is a whippet?" I finally asked. Henry and Orlando laughed.

Headed back to the car, we spotted this large painting of Larry from the Three Stooges—Larry Fine, a Philly native—with his signature crazy hair. We couldn't resist. We circled up in front of the painting and snapped a selfie to send to Larry Titus. We texted it to him, "Hey Larry! Thinking of you!"

He replied, "Wise guys!"

One more Philly recollection ...

A few months earlier, I'd had an emotional—and comical—visit with Henry on his home turf. It was during a trip I made back to Pennsylvania with my friend Richard. We'd be meeting our friend and collaborative writer Darin and his wife, Shari, over in Mill City for the weekend, planning for the release of

Unshackled.

Richard and I landed in Philly and rented a car for the drive to my sister Mary's place. We put on the GPS to make our way to the highway. Richard mentioned Philadelphia's claim to fame—the Philly Cheesesteak sandwich.

I'd learned from Henry that at the heart of the Philly Cheesesteak legend is an infamous battle between Pat's and Gino's as to just *whose* cheesesteak sandwich is *the one* Philly is famous for. Richard said he'd like to try them both. *It was lunchtime.* The next thing I knew, we were reprogramming our GPS to find both Pat's *and* Gino's.

You know how it goes with a GPS—a female voice is telling you, "In two-tenths of a mile, turn left on ..." We were blindly following along when I looked up and saw a Catholic church on a corner. Suddenly I realized, *This place looks awful familiar to me.* Instinctively, I told Richard, "Hang a left here."

Then I knew for sure; I'd been here before. Maybe six months earlier, I had flown up for Henry's re-sentencing hearing. I rode to court that day with Henry's sister, and we stopped to pick up their mother on the way. This was *that* neighborhood. Henry was released on parole some 45 days after that hearing and was staying at his mom's house. *We were on Henry's street!*

I recognized the house. We pulled up in front and I dialed Henry's phone number. "Hey man! We're here!"

"You're where?" he asked.

"Here! Look out the window."

I heard the phone drop, and 20 seconds later, Henry burst out the front door and jumped down the steps to us. We hugged it out! I'm so grateful Richard had the presence of mind to capture the emotional moment on his phone. I posted on social media, and as often as it comes up in my memories, I revisit that video and smile.

Of course, we asked Henry to join us on our cheesesteak quest. He's such a prankster—he told us that he's loyal to Pat's, so he couldn't be seen going into Gino's. "I'm a Pat's guy. This is serious," he said. He teased us that he'd need to cross the street and pretend he didn't know us if we went into Gino's.

Henry did educate us foreigners, "You don't say cheesesteak, you say 'wit cheese.' Not *with*, but *wit*."

When in Philly, do as the locals—so I walked up to the counter and told the guys in white t-shirts, "wit cheese."

We tried Gino's first. Then Pat's. Turns out, I'm a Pat's guy too.

CHAPTER 2

FREEDOM

The walk of shame—it's that one-block walk from the holding cell at one end of Clay Street in Tunkhannock to the Wyoming County Courthouse at the other, dressed in a prison jumpsuit, cuffed and shackled, escorted by deputies, all under the watchful eye of neighborhood residents out collecting their morning papers and walking their dogs. The deputies were taking me to Courtroom 2; the very courtroom where I'd been sentenced 34 years earlier to life without the possibility of parole.

Coming out of the courthouse after my hearing however, *as a free man*, was a totally different experience. I had to walk back up the street to the jail to be processed out—still wearing an orange jumpsuit—but this time without the cuffs and shackles ... *and with lilt in my step*. I felt like dancing up that street!

In no time at all, now fully out-processed and dressed in the street clothes my sister, Mary, had gathered for me—and doused with *Dolce Gabbana Light Blue* cologne to the point your eyes would water—I stepped back out onto Clay Street. Friends and family rushed to embrace me.

An entire crowd of people, many I didn't even recognize, wanted to shake my hand, hug and congratulate me. I really couldn't tell you who all and what all—it was just this most wonderful, tears-of-joy-inducing crush of love and support. At one point someone handed me a phone to call Larry. I ended up getting his voicemail, an entirely unknown experience to me. Imagining I was talking to one of those old tape-recorder answering machines sitting on a kitchen counter, I started saying "Hey, Larry? Dad! If you're there, pick up!"

People were telling me, "Leave a message." Larry saved a copy of the recording—it's really funny!

Somebody said, "Let's pray, because we have lunch reservations at the Country Club." And pray we did! Those precious moments were captured on an iPad and several phones—it brings tears to my eyes every time I revisit those images.

We moved like a herd toward the cars, and I made my way into my brother-in-law Joe's truck. Climbing in, my first thought: *This truck is amazing!* Plush interior, high-tech sound system, climate control—*pickup trucks sure had changed over 35 years!* And the ride itself—all the sights and sounds—I sat, eyes-fixed out the window, taking in all the wonders of a perfect spring Pennsylvania afternoon. The colors and beauty, the homes with manicured lawns and gardens, cars on the road, people out and about, living—all things we so often take for granted.

A crowd awaited us at the restaurant. They had an area set up for our party—maybe 20 or so people were already seated when I arrived. It was so special to look around the room and see all these friends and loved ones here for me. Because we were among the last to arrive, Marty and Nataley had ordered on my behalf: eggs benedict and Canadian bacon were on the way.

Eating hadn't even crossed my mind really. I was still in take-it-all-in mode. When I sat down, the first thing I noticed was my table service, and how heavy the fork felt in my hand. Plus, there was a big steak knife with a wooden handle next to my plate. I hadn't seen a steak knife in a very long time. *That's not prison plastic-ware!*

When my plate arrived, it looked like something you'd see in a magazine. *That's not prison food!* And my first bite confirmed it—may have been the best meal I'd ever had. I took my time, savoring every bite. My entire meal experience was like this, right down to when I had finished.

I told our server, "You can take my tray."

Nataley giggled ... "That is a plate, not a tray. You're not in prison anymore."

After the meal, Nataley wanted to show me her new Honda. We walked out and I sat down inside; it seemed like a rocket-ship to me with its space-age-looking console and instruments. For the ride over to Mary's house, I jumped into Rob's Range Rover. Like Joe's truck and Nataley's Civic, I couldn't get over how nice and high-tech automobiles had gotten over the years. With that old 1960s four-door Rambler we had when I was a kid, comfort was a plastic cup-holder hanging from the armrest; the sound system was an AM radio ... and good luck with reception. Climate control? If you got hot, *roll down the window*! If you got cold, *roll it up*!

The closer we got to Mary's place, the more memories came flooding back. My sister lived within walking distance of the house where we'd grown up. Not a lot had changed. I recognized where we were as we drove down roads we'd walked as kids to catch the school bus. I had flashbacks of hitch-hiking in the rain to get to some girl's house ... *and catching a ride from a cop*!

Pulling into Mary's place, things looked familiar even though I'd never been there before. Mom had sent me pictures years earlier when they were building: photos of her place at the bottom of the driveway, and Mary and Joe's home up at the top.

A lot of people dropped by Mary's house that afternoon and evening to see me—I can't even tell you who all stopped in. It was just so cool for me to be able to circulate among people, to freely walk in and out, to be able to step outside as often as I wanted to enjoy the fresh air.

My nephew, Mark, got a cell phone for me. He set out to teach me how to use it; how to call, text and take pictures. It was information overload for me. Does anyone else remember when telephones were ... *telephones*? Things sure had come a long way since the old kitchen-wall phone and extra-long coiled cord I grew up with.

Although the hour grew late, I was wide awake. It was as if I didn't want my first night of freedom to end. It was all still sinking in: *I could go anywhere I wanted, do anything I felt like doing.* There would be no lockdown order coming. No unit, no cell, no bunk. But rather a comfortable guestroom bed at my sister's home was turned down and waiting for me. I was just in no hurry to get there.

I slid the glass door open and stepped outside. I sat down in a lawn chair under the stars. The sights, sounds and scents of nature enveloped me. It was a cool night, so I was wrapped up in a blanket. I sat there all night just looking up at the stars through tear-filled eyes, thanking and praising my Father.

It got to be about 5 a.m. Everyone was asleep, but I was bouncing off the walls! *What can I do on my first full day of freedom?* I grabbed my new phone and called Doc. Doc was a friend and fellow inmate at SCI Rockview. He'd been released a year or so before me. He lived maybe 15 or 20 miles from Mary.

I'd met Doc years earlier when he came to church one day out of the blue. I was a greeter that day. I really enjoyed being a greeter because I had a passion for welcoming guys at the door and giving them a positive first impression. I introduced myself and asked, "What's your name?"

"Doc," he replied. I invited him in and did my best to make sure he felt right at home. I was thrilled when he returned the following week. I announced, "Doc is in the house!" to which he laughed. He eventually came to faith in Jesus. Sometime later he shared that he kept coming back to church because "Gene remembered my name."

He picked up and I said, "Hey Doc! It's Gene!" The time hadn't dawned on me—I mean, it *was* after 5 a.m. In prison, 5 in the morning and you're up! Doc didn't know I was out. He was surprised to hear my voice on the phone, particularly because my call didn't begin with the usual operator's voice saying, "This is a pre-paid call from an inmate at SCI Rockview."

He immediately told me, "I'll come get you."

We were a few years older now, but Doc hadn't changed much—into his 60s, he's still got those GQ-model looks: tall, handsome, clean-shaven, chiseled face, a full head of hair cut short and salted with gray. I spent a good part of the day with him. He was doing great, too. It was awesome to catch up. We still keep in touch. He has a Gospel group now; I saw him at a *Music on the Lawn* event in Lake Winola, not long ago.

It had been another full day of activity, but I was still stir-crazy at 10 p.m. I asked Mary, "Can I go to the mall?"

She laughed. "First, there's no mall around here. There is a 24-hour Walmart. Second, you don't have to ask for permission! You're free! See if Mark will take you."

On the way out the door to Walmart, Mark grabbed his wallet and keys and said we'd need to stop for gas. We pulled into the little gas-and-convenience store down the road. As Mark was pumping, a car pulled in real fast and a young lady jumped out, approached us and said, "Hey! Can you help me? I came to buy cigarettes but forgot my ID."

"Sorry," Mark said. "I don't have my wallet." I knew he did. Then she turned to me.

"How about you?"

"I just got out of prison today. I don't even have an ID."

"Oh!" she replied. "How long were you in for?" ... to which I answered, "A long time."

She asked again, "How long?" so I told her. She jumped back in her car and sped off.

Mark said, "I've seen her pull this ruse before. She's not 18."

It started me thinking, though—I'd need an ID. *How do you get one? And how long does it take?* Thankfully, this was a detail Mary hadn't overlooked. The very next morning, we were on our way to the DMV.

Tunkhannock's Department of Motor Vehicles was crowded. There were several lines, each one deep with people holding fistfuls of forms and documentation, patiently awaiting their turn. And here I was, my forms in hand to procure a State of Pennsylvania non-drivers identification card. Mary and my niece, Stephanie, waited with me.

I was filled with nervous energy waiting for the line to move. I hadn't slept the night before; really, I hadn't slept much at all in the days leading up to my release. And now, here I was—my very first day ... free. I looked around in wonder. *I'm free!*

A tall, athletic-looking guy standing just ahead of us in line turned around, smiled and extended his hand, saying, "Welcome home!" He introduced himself and his daughter. "You may not remember me, but we went to high school together. I was a year ahead of you. I read the newspaper article about your release yesterday, and I just wanted to say I'm really happy for you."

Mary smiled and gave me a hug. She knew that this man's words brought comfort to me. I had no idea how people might react, or if they would react at all. Some 35 years had passed. Would people remember? *What* would they remember?

A few more minutes of waiting and soon I was standing before the clerk. She reviewed my documents and directed me to stand in front of the camera— and this time I wasn't holding up a mug-shot template and prisoner number. This time I wore a smile.

Next, we were on our way to meet Jim Neary and his probation office staff to thank them for all the work they had done in securing my release. We stopped at a flower shop on the way; I picked out some flowers for Cindy, one of Jim's assistants, who had worked tirelessly with Mary to get all my life papers and identification needs in order, dotting every "i" and crossing every "t." Jim had nicknamed the two of them Co-Chairs of the Identification Committee.

I am so grateful for Jim and Cindy, and all the dear people in their office. They became champions for me and my case. I didn't realize it at the time it was happening, but so many components went into my release, most of which I wasn't privy to and didn't see. They worked tirelessly behind the scenes on my behalf. I'm overwhelmed to think about what it must have taken for a judge to decide to throw out my life sentence and release me after 35 years, and to just let me walk out the door a free man! Even my own attorney cautioned me not to get my hopes up, figuring if I was going to be released at all it would probably involve moving into a halfway house or residential program. He said plainly: "Judges don't outright release *anyone* after such a long period of incarceration."

Well, God made it happen. A Him-credible miracle. And these people were the instruments He used to pull it off.

It was wonderful to visit with Cindy, Jim and his staff. Joyous laughter flowed—and you get the feeling in a probation office that this was a special victory for one and all. We went exuberantly back and forth, recalling how the hearing unfolded from each of our unique emotional vantage points. Someone asked me what I was thinking as the judge read his order. *I was doing math!* When Judge Shurtleff said the maximum sentence was "34 years, nine months, and 15 days," I was hard at work trying to figure out ... *How close am I?* Then pandemonium broke out—camera clicks and flashes ... shouts ... joy!

"He never closed the session," Jim said. "Judge Shurtleff never dismissed the court." Everyone reflected on that for a moment—he was right. Not one of us remembers him closing the hearing.

"I've never seen anything like it before," Jim explained. "I'm sure it was emotional for him, too. He just watched for a moment, stood up, turned and walked out. And the court reporter ... she was looking around like, *Is it over?* Tears filled her eyes. After a moment or two, she gathered her things and slipped out."

After we arrived home that afternoon, I was sitting out on the deck enjoying the sun and giving thanks. Mary stepped out to join me. "Jim Neary just called," she told me. "He said you were the first person in 32 years of his career who had ever returned to his office to say 'thank you.'"

Tears filled my eyes, and my thoughts drifted to the one leper who returned to thank Jesus after He'd healed 10 of them.

I made a promise to Jim and his staff—a promise I've made in my heart to Judge Shurtleff, to all of the people who've stood with me and to all my guys still doing time—*I won't let them down.* This isn't some in-the-flesh promise; this is a commitment borne of God's mercy and grace and by the power of my Lord Jesus Christ.

Over the next few days, I spent a lot of time with my childhood friend Bill Nast, his wife, Karen, and their daughters, Jordyn and Emily. The Nasts own a beautiful piece of property some 45 minutes away, where they run a ministry called Grace & Glory Outreach. Bill asked if I'd do Grace & Glory's Easter Sunday service. I was honored and overwhelmed at God's goodness once again—I'd probably spent more time with Bill growing up than anyone else. Over the years since, he and Karen and the girls visited me regularly at Rockview.

When he'd visit, I'd say, "I'm gonna be released someday." Bill will tell you, in his heart he doubted it. As much a man of faith that Bill is, he'd also worked for many years in the prison system. He knew that the doors were getting closed tighter and tighter; the way things were going, commutations were fewer and farther between. And now, to be here on his property, talking and laughing about it all in retrospect, was priceless. God is so good!

Easter 2012 was one I'll never forget. It was quite a celebration. There were probably 45 or 50 people at the Grace & Glory Outreach Church service and picnic that day—some local, some from farther away, and maybe 10 or 12 people I knew from high school. This was my first time sharing the Gospel as a free man. It was electrifying! Lots of laughs. Lots of tears. The feeling in my heart of *I'm doing exactly what God has for me to do at this moment* is tremendous. I could feel the power of the Holy Spirit in our midst.

. . .

The following weekend I visited Rob's new home, a beautiful piece of property he'd bought and named Rak'd Up Lodge. I suppose it was a couple of months before my release that Rob had first told me about this place, describing the long driveway that led to a cabin with a wrap-around porch, perched on 150 acres of land, with expansive views; and the property's biggest draw was his neighbors—deer and wild turkeys.

Rob had a vision to launch an executive retreat center. I had said on the phone call, "So you're thinking of buying this land?"

And he responded, "I already did!" Just before our 15 minutes was up—a real drawback of those prison telephone conversations is the time limit, and the automated voice reminding you, "You have one minute left"—Rob hurried to say, "I can't wait to show you this place when you get out."

Driving onto the property, the place was even more beautiful than I'd imagined it. The driveway was lined on both sides with tall blue spruces, and it opened to this gorgeous, picturesque setting: a brown log cabin with thick, white stone chimneys—one on each side—a spacious wrap-around porch overlooking about 10 acres of field that had been plowed, ready to be planted with corn ... it was like something you'd see in a magazine. I could imagine his dream of a retreat center. I could picture all the wonderful, soul-impacting work that God would do here. Not to mention, this place was quite a contrast to my home for the last 35 years—a 9x7 cell.

Every experience was like this for me—like brand-new. The hour-long ride out there in Rob's Range Rover, for instance, with our butts nestled into plush seats and the stereo blasting Rascal Flatts, was quite a contrast from a ride on the old Blue Goose prison van—an old school bus painted blue with hard bench seats and metal screens welded over the windows. That, by the way, was my first prison job: welding. I was one of the guys who put those screens on the Blue Goose!

We sat for a good while on his porch together, reflecting on God's goodness and faithfulness. We reminisced over the years behind us—Rob started visiting me at Camp Hill way back in 1987. Every Wednesday the officer in the Visitor's Shack would call down to the inmate housing unit: "AK4192 McGuire, you have a visitor!" I'd hear that and run back to my cell to wash my face, brush my teeth and put on some deodorant (there's just about nothing worse than BO or bad breath, all-too-often the norm among inmates).

We talked about the past few months leading up to my release, marveling over all the details that had fallen into place and everything that happened in the courtroom; nothing could be explained away as anything other than the handiwork of God. I pulled a folded copy of the judge's order out of my pocket and began to read it again: *THE ORDER OF THE COURT: AND NOW, April 3, 2012, the defendant, Eugene McGuire, is sentenced to pay the cost of the prosecution and be committed to the Department of Corrections for confinement in a state institution for a period of not less than fifteen (15) years nor more than thirty-four (34) years, nine (9) months and fifteen (15) days, and stand committed until the same complied with.*

We both were crying like babies.

"You hungry?" Rob asked. "I've got some chicken marinating. I can toss it on the grill. It'll be ready in a few minutes." Sounded great to me. And yet another experience to treasure—such a departure from the routine I'd been accustomed to: a block sergeant shouting over the PA system, "Meal line going out, men! Five minutes on the door! Five minutes on the door!"

A truck appeared, heading up the driveway. "That's my John Deere!" Rob shouted. He'd mentioned earlier that he bought a tractor to prepare the fields for planting, to plow and bale some hay. I guess I'd imagined a little cub-sized thing, but as this flatbed truck came into view, the machine it carried was huge!

"You weren't joking when you said you ordered a tractor," I said.

A short man with an Amish beard, no moustache and a Moe-looking haircut exited the truck and started toward us. Rob introduced himself: "Hi. I'm Rob Meier."

The man answered, his accent heavy Pennsylvania Dutch; "Pleasure to meet you. My name is Elam." He must have read confusion on both our faces, because he quickly clarified, "That's 'male' spelled backwards. My mother named me." A big smile broke out above his Amish beard.

Rob introduced me. Elam looked us over and asked, "Are you two brothers?" The words rolled off Elam's tongue very deliberately, like he was speaking in slow-motion.

Rob smiled at me and answered, "Sort of. We're Christian brothers." Elam nodded. And then Rob being Rob, you know what came next: "Gene has been away for a while. This is his first day here."

Again, with the drawl, Elam asked, "Where were you? In prison?"

Rob and I were both shocked. *Did he actually just ask that?* Elam pointed to my haircut, a standard high-and-tight, and said, "You were either in prison or in the military. So how long were you in for?"

I answered, "35 years. I just got out 15 days ago."

Elam nodded again, "What'd you do? Kill somebody?" We almost fell over! "That amount of time," Elam explained, "our church does some prison ministry, and guys I've met with that amount of time in have usually killed somebody."

Rob spoke up. "Gene spent 34 years, nine months and 15 days incarcerated for a murder his cousin committed while they were out drinking one night. Gene was just 17 when they gave him a life sentence."

Elam looked me in the eye and said, "The mill of God grinds slow, but exceedingly fine."

The man soon set out to unload Rob's tractor and ensure everything operated properly. The work done and delivery order signed, Rob offered, "Would you like to break some bread with us?" Elam seemed confused by the phrase, so Rob clarified, "Would you care to join us for lunch?" Over the course of the next hour or so, we ate and enjoyed some very warm fellowship. Plenty of testimonies and prayers were shared.

When Elam left, Rob and I reflected on the experience—a stranger, a brother in Christ, such meaningful but measured words, keen in perception, drenched in grace, blessing us with pearls of wisdom, encouraging us ... and all as he came to deliver a tractor. God is so good! And sometimes that goodness is revealed in and through the most random of occasions.

It is not lost on me that I'm writing of this man, Elam, and our one-time encounter as a truly blessed memory from the early days of my freedom. Not to mention my little Amish brother's wisdom: "The mill of God grinds slow, but exceedingly fine" continues to speak to my heart.

Going to Texas and working with the Tituses seemed like a no-brainer. Larry had been a pastor, mentor and friend to me all these years.

It was a Sunday morning early in 2011 when Larry and his wife, Devi, were both sitting in Chaplain Reitz's office at SCI Rockview. Pastor Larry was there to conduct the worship service. Some 250 men were crammed into the chapel. Everyone familiar with Larry's ministry was really excited to hear him speak, especially me.

My *Post Conviction Relief Act* paperwork filed with the Wyoming County Court, I was waiting for Judge Shurtleff to set a hearing date. Devi asked, "Gene, what do you plan to do once you are released?" My answer was a simple: "I want to move to Dallas and work in ministry."

Devi looked at Larry, and they both smiled. "Well," Larry said, "I believe we can raise a small salary for you for the first year."

"And you can stay in our home," Devi offered, "until you are able to afford your own apartment." Just like that, I had a plan.

I'd love to tell you it was some deep spiritual leading that had me convinced Dallas was the place for me. Honestly, the Cowboys had a lot to do with it. I'd been a Cowboys fan all my life. Of course, Larry and Devi living and ministering in Texas for six years was the real draw—it felt like the place to be and the ministry to be a part of. I believed my best footing for starting a new season of my life would be living and working closely with Larry.

Later in 2011, the court heard my case. The DA agreed with my attorney's brief, and just a few months later, come February 2012, the judge vacated my life sentence, ordering me to appear in my hometown courthouse on April 3, 2012.

Ironically, the Tituses were traveling to Brazil for a missions conference on the day of my release. They had filed a document with the court detailing their intention to provide a home and job for me in Texas. After a few weeks of staying with my sister and reconnecting with family and friends in Pennsylvania, I'd be on my way to the Lone Star State.

Rob offered to help get me there. He assured me, however, "If you ever decide you'd rather stay here in Pennsylvania, I've got room for you." It was a very attractive offer, as I have family and friends in PA whom I love dearly. But I couldn't shake the idea of a fresh start in Texas.

Rob was good with my decision, yet he reminded me often that his "offer still stands." He went a long way to comfort Mary, reminding her how "Gene will only be a few hours away, and he is a free man. He can come and go as he pleases." Being reminded of this—of my new freedom—was special for sure.

The big day arrived. My flight to Texas was an amazing experience. Rob arranged the entire trip. He hooked us up with a limo ride to the airport and seats in first class—*Wow!* "Nothing but the best for Gene McGuire—a free man!" Rob teased.

We sat down in the plane's first row. A beautiful, gracious, brown-eyed flight attendant welcomed us, asking, "Would you like something to drink?"

Rob ordered a Bloody Mary. She looked at me and asked, "And for you, sir?"

I must have hesitated—and of course Rob seized the moment: "Oh, that's right! They didn't offer you those where you were at, did they?" I laughed. Our flight attendant looked puzzled.

Rob explained, "My best friend here has an amazing story." Her brown eyes grew bigger. "Gene spent 34 years, nine months and 15 days in prison for a murder he didn't commit. But now he's a free man."

She smiled and indicated she'd like to hear more of my story, but she had other passengers to attend to and tasks to complete to prepare for take-off.

Mid-flight, she motioned to me to join her in the plane's galley. I shared a little of my story with her, and she told me a little of her own. She'd been in a terrible car accident that left her with a serious head injury; she was in a coma for more than a month. We realized we'd both experienced a miracle of God's redeeming love, that He rescued our lives from the depths.

From the little bowl of cashews they handed me as I boarded through a pretty awesome in-flight meal and right up to the warm towels they handed out to freshen us up before we landed, my first class flight experience was most memorable. And the chance connection with our flight attendant, sharing my testimony and being blessed to hear hers, was priceless.

When we arrived in Texas, Larry and Devi were there to greet us. It felt unbelievable to be there; free from confinement and free to make choices and live the new life the Lord had given me. I must have looked like a kid in a candy store—I was overwhelmed everywhere I looked.

First of all, it's true what they say about Texas: *Everything is big!* Land. Stores. Parking lots. Cowboy hats. Steaks. Four-wheel drive pickup trucks— *Cowboy Cadillacs*!

I was pretty mesmerized just looking out the car window as we traveled to the Titus' home. All the lawns, hedges and gardens were neatly trimmed, clean and tight. It was like driving through an upscale real estate magazine's pages. I started noticing the vehicles that weren't big pickup trucks and SUVs: a lot of really nice Mercedes and Lexus automobiles. "Welcome to Colleyville," Devi said.

The Titus' home is gorgeous. It has two guest suites, so I'd have my own bedroom and bathroom. If I had any question about how marvelous the Lord's provision could be, or how much He loved me, this place cleared it up. Unbelievable! I thought, *I wish the guys back at Rockview could see me now.*

My first night in Texas, they took me into Fort Worth to a place called Joe T. Garcia's. You've got to see this place to believe it. Let's just say seeing it fresh off 34 years, 9 months and 15 days in the care of the Pennsylvania Department of Corrections offers quite a perspective. This place seemed like the eighth Wonder of the World to me. Two blocks of festive, outdoor dining among elaborate gardens and inviting water fountains with a mariachi band strolling around. More special memories being made with special people—dear friends, brothers and sisters in Christ—and all experiences beyond my wildest dreams. I was simply in awe: *Now to him who is able to do immeasurably more than all we ask or imagine, according to his power that is at work within us, to him be glory in the church and in Christ Jesus throughout all generations, for ever and ever!* Amen.

I started my new job in the offices of Kingdom Global Ministry the next day. Walking into the KGM office for the first time was an experience I'd never imagined, and one I'll never forget. I was greeted with applause and even a few hoots and hollers—this is Texas!

I never realized the staff there felt like they knew me; they'd all heard so much about me from the Titus family. I'd actually spoken to several of these people on the telephone over the years; Larry instructed the staff to always accept collect calls from the prison, even if he wasn't in to take them personally. I was embraced with hugs and smiles. It felt great to be welcomed and celebrated.

This feeling takes me back to the surprise birthday parties we used to throw for our friends in the prison. Somebody would keep the birthday boy occupied while everyone else decorated his cell with toilet paper and string and stuff. We'd all pitch in, bust open a box of Little Debbies from the commissary, stick some match sticks in them for candles, all just to say, "We care about you." That is how this welcome at KGM felt; *these people cared about me.*

It was a wonderful welcome. Then came a bit of a reality check—it was time to work. I had an office, which was sort of a glorified storage closet. There was a desk, a small file cabinet and a plant. I had a telephone with all sorts of lines and buttons and an intercom—none of which made any sense to me. Telephones had changed quite a bit over 35 years!

Larry introduced me to a really nice lady named Cindy, whose job it would be to help me acclimate to office life. She'd teach me things like data processing. *Help me, Jesus!* I'd never used computers before. "Cindy's going to teach you," Larry said. But all I could think was, *This poor lady! Lord Jesus, help Cindy!*

She asked me, "Are you familiar with Google?"

I was like, "Isn't that where you go to get eyeglasses?..."

The Tituses are driven ministers. As such, they are very intentional about *all* aspects of their lives and schedules. Everything is pretty regimented. Their household routines were a challenge for me—they expected everyone at the table for meals; everything was done throughout the day at set times and in a certain manner. I hadn't considered how much living with, working with and spending all of your free time with the same people, on such a regimented routine and schedule, could start to feel a little like prison. I found myself, some days, resenting the formality. Every once in a while, I thought how awesome it would be to just eat a bowl of cereal standing at the kitchen counter, looking out the window … and then dropping the bowl in the sink, running a little water over it and going for a morning run. But that's not how things were done in the Titus household.

I want to be very clear: Larry and Devi never said or did anything to make me feel uncomfortable. It's just that when someone does as much for you as they have done for me, it becomes really hard to say, "I'm sorry you made plans for me tonight, but I already have plans of my own." I appreciated everything they'd done and were continuing to do. And everything was fantastic! But I had a desire to get away from them a bit, too.

If I'm being completely honest, while this office gig they'd provided *was* ministry, it's not a side of ministry I'd ever considered. Ministry, as I'd experienced it, involved spending time face-to-face with people, listening, caring and praying. Where the rubber meets the road. This office work was the back-end of ministry, the administrative side of things. I understood it as necessary, but it wasn't where I'd imagined serving. It wasn't where I felt entirely comfortable serving. It certainly didn't feel like this was where and how I was skilled to serve. With my lack of office acumen, it felt like I sat there day after day while they all tried to find something … *anything* … for me to do.

I started to realize ministry in an office, at a desk, wasn't for me.

One aspect of working at KGM that I really did enjoy, however, was the weekly prayer meeting and the chance it offered me to meet up afterward with guys like Pastor Chris Baer for coffee and doughnuts across the street. I loved hearing what God was doing in and through Chris' ministry. I loved praying and sharing together. This sort of interaction was much more where my heart wanted to be.

Larry has a real burden to train up men for leadership. He's ministered to men all across America and around the world. Discovering I wasn't a fit for office work, and realizing how much I loved connecting one-on-one with other believers, sharing and praying, Larry asked if I'd be willing to start reaching out to men who had attended one of his Teleios Summits by following up with encouraging calls and emails. I agreed ... and enjoyed this task immensely. I loved hearing updates on their lives and ministry. We'd pray together. Sometimes I'd get to share the elevator version of my own testimony. Then they'd pray for me. More than a few times, we'd plan to meet up for lunch or coffee. Meeting guys and then spending time together—this is ministry for me! Unfortunately, it was only a small part of my job at KGM.

The Titus family and my time at KGM were absolute blessings provided by the Lord's hand. I was grateful for their plan and the chance to earn a $1,500-a-month salary and save toward a car while staying in their home. But something in my heart was changing, and no amount of prayer was quelling the desire *to be somewhere else and to do something different.*

When I was in prison, I dreamed of pastoring a church one day. It was my sole passion while I was incarcerated. The thought of a career where you pray and study all week, then share the Word and fellowship with others, thrilled me. I'd been an assistant to Chaplain Reitz, helped out with worship, discipleship, mentoring. Pastoring seemed like the next logical step for me.

Larry and Devi had the same thought. Often at breakfast, Devi shared what she believed God's will for me included. She'd say she saw me sharing an apartment with Felipe (the Titus' administrative assistant and Portuguese translator), starting a Bible study in our apartment complex and having it grow into a church. She even suggested a church name. But I was moving away from that picture in my heart, not toward it.

I love Felipe. He's a dear friend. But I'd just spent 35 years living with cellies. I wasn't feeling the whole *roommate* situation. And my vision for pastoring a church was changing, too. I'd been attending Gateway, a massive church with five campuses and 30,000-plus in weekly attendance. And to get to Gateway on Sunday, I'd drive past a dozen or so other expansive churches—mega-churches on every corner. I began to wonder: *Why in the world would Dallas need yet another church?*

Sometimes knowing what you *don't* want to do will clear the way for you to recognize what you *do* want to do.

At the same time, I was receiving offers from several men's ministries to come and share my story, to bring a message from the Word and to relate to the men in person—*and I loved every opportunity I got*! I could see God's anointing on this ministry, and the impact that my story—which is really *His* story—was having on people's lives. It finally dawned on me: *This is my calling.*

I phoned my friend Rob and talked with him both about my struggles at KGM and my excitement in these new ministering opportunities. He lovingly reminded me, "You've always got a place here in Pennsylvania!" And I appreciated knowing that, but I also knew Texas was where I was supposed to be.

We prayed together several times over the phone. Rob kept asking me, "What is the Lord saying to you?" I had always felt an evangelistic calling. I knew I wanted to share my testimony. I also knew that it didn't matter to me whether I was sharing across a table, over a cup of coffee, one-on-one or before a large crowd at a men's conference—*I just needed to tell people about Jesus*. Rob encouraged me that God would make a way; God would open a door.

Then, one morning as I was out in the car with Larry getting a driving lesson, that door appeared.

Imagine this if you've ever taught a teenager how to drive an automobile: I was 52 years old, settling in behind the wheel of a car to learn the rules of the road. Mid-lesson, Larry spoke up, "I've noticed you're not enjoying working in the office." I admitted it was true. He then asked, "Are you thinking of moving back to Pennsylvania?"

I told Larry I was sure that my future was in Texas, but that I needed to find something else to do. Larry graciously opened the door: "Well, since you're not happy at the office, why don't you talk to James about a job?"

When he said this, I wondered if he and James had spoken about me. I'd really enjoyed spending time with James—Larry's son-in-law—on weekends. In fact, James and Trina had even asked me, "How's the office work at Kingdom Global going?" They both knew the answer without me even saying it—*it wasn't.* James had offered, more than a few times, "You ought to come work with me in roofing." Maybe it was time for a change.

"You and Devi have done so much for me," I told Larry. "I don't want to disappoint you." He assured me—like a father would—that whatever I decided to do, he wouldn't be disappointed. He was committed to me. The following day, I penned my first ever two weeks' notice resignation letter.

My last several days at KGM were bittersweet. I sent emails and letters of appreciation out to the dozens of friends who had been supporting me financially through KGM, informing them that I'd be moving on. Larry, Devi and Felipe were headed off for a month of ministry in Brazil. By the time they'd return, I'd be moved out of the Titus home and into a small mother-in-law apartment attached to James and Trina's house ... and looking for work.

CHAPTER 3

NEW MERCIES

James set up a lunchtime meeting for me. "You'll love Monty when you meet him," he promised. I nodded, bouncing my head in time with the Phil Wickham song on the radio.

James had worked as a contractor for Monty's roofing business for a few years, repairing storm-damaged buildings. James dialed his son, Brandon. "Hey, can you meet us at Anamia's? Gene and I are having lunch with Monty." I really looked forward to seeing Brandon again.

I'd first met Brandon when he was a little kid, way back when I was incarcerated at Camp Hill, like '87 or '88. When Larry would come see me, James often came in with him, spending time with some of the other guys. He'd usually bring Brandon along. One of the guys James came to see regularly was Albert. I mentioned Albert in *Unshackled* (he spent a few hours hiding *under* my bunk during the Camp Hill riots of 1989). Albert was great with kids—he's like a big kid himself. He'd hoist four-year-old Brandon up on his shoulders, and they'd be giggling and carrying on. Childish joy! Fun!

Looking back, those visits meant the world to me. To all of us. On Christmas mornings, especially, I remember Larry would come and bring his whole family; they'd have Christmas with us before going back home to have their own family Christmas. This spoke volumes to the guys. To know these folks cared about us, wanted to be with us—you just felt Jesus' love in that.

Brandon is all grown up now, of course, and working for his dad. I remember back in the day thinking that young Brandon was just like a miniature version of his dad. Seeing the adult version of that relationship today sure is sweet.

As we pulled into Anamia's parking lot, James asked, "Have you ever eaten here before?"

"No. This will be another first for me!"

And let me tell you, what a *fantastic* first!

We walked in and the place was unbelievable. Fancy? Everything was new and shiny—just beautiful. And authentic Tex-Mex. The atmosphere, the food, the service—it was all excellent. It was hard to get over the fact that *just a few weeks earlier* I was eating in a prison chow-hall. At this point, I was still following people's advice on what to order and watching with wonder as other people's plates were going by—*Wow! What's that?* And I mean that in a very different sense from the *Uh ... what is THAT?* you'd often hear on taco night in the chow-hall ... pondering the brown smear of meat-like substance on a tortilla.

For a few weeks, now, James had been telling me about the amount of work he was coming into through Monty's company. There had been major hailstorms across Oklahoma; golf ball-sized hail punched through roofs of private residences, businesses, churches and schools. The need was tremendous.

(I'd asked James once how he got started in roofing. He explained that his opportunity to go out and sell roofing for Monty came about around the time Hurricane Katrina decimated the Gulf Coast. He shared how difficult it was for him to approach people in such need. He would feel frozen at first. Sitting in his truck one day, he prayed, "I don't think I can do this, Lord! I can't *sell* roofing!" But James heard God say, "I'm not asking you to sell roofing. I'm asking you to knock on their doors and ask how you can help them." James took that word to heart. And you can see this in the way he goes about his job—as important as fixing someone's roof the right way is to James, encouraging the hearts of people who've been devastated by life's storms is far more important. This is *his* ministry. That first day, God moved James far beyond feeling frozen ... and he signed 30 contracts. God is blessing James' business. James is blessing others.

That's a formula for success. *That* is ministry the way God intends it!)

Because James told me Monty's company was so busy, I imagined this lunchtime meeting might end up becoming a job opportunity. Perhaps this was the Lord's next step for me—my first step away from KGM.

Monty and Brandon were already there when James and I arrived. And my first take on Monty? He looked just like the wrestler, Stone Cold Steve Austin. Big. Muscular. Shaved head. I could totally imagine him narrowing his stare at the camera and saying, "And that's the bottom line, 'cuz Stone Cold says so!"

Between the chips and guacamole and our main courses arriving, I shared my story. I found myself especially emotional as I got to April 3, 2012, about how the judge ordered me released and friends and family in the courtroom erupted. Pandemonium! I named my first book after this very moment, as someone shouted, "Unshackle that man!"

As I was telling the story to Monty, I really flashed back there emotionally. I vividly remembered collapsing into sobs; how my sister, Mary, quite literally climbed over courtroom furniture to reach me; how I hollered out, "Thank you, Your Honor!" ... and only learned later that the judge had never closed the session and dismissed the court; how, amidst all the emotion, he slipped out leaving even his stenographer wondering, *Is it over?* It was, indeed. Jesus said, "It is finished!"

I get emotional telling this part of the story pretty often, as you can imagine. But this day it really stirred me deep. I looked up through my tears and noticed Monty's eyes were tear-filled also. James was wiping his eyes. Brandon, too. And yet, we were all smiling! Ear-to-ear, at God's goodness! Joy! A real anointing! I wonder what the servers thought when they rolled up on our table with our plates of sizzling hot fajitas to find four grown men crying like babies.

One reason I get emotional in re-telling this part of my story is that the further I'm removed from that day, the more I see how God's goodness and provision had gone out before me. I stood there *unshackled*, but also facing a great *unknown*. He'd been faithful to provide for me each step of the way. Even in those times when I had no idea what He was thinking—looking back over those five commutation denials, for instance—I still knew in my heart, God's got this!

Now, I had new questions—*Should I stay at Kingdom Global? Would there be another opportunity?* The same way God had me all the way through those 34 years, nine months and 15 days, I knew He had me now.

We finished lunch. Stuffed! "Let's head back to my office," Monty said. "Gene, you ride with me." Yet again, it's true what they say about everything being bigger in Texas. Walking toward Monty's truck, I couldn't help but giggle. Big truck for a big man. Ford Super Duty, all jacked up. I'd just about need a boost to climb in.

On the ride, Monty shared a little of his story, including that he had a brother who was incarcerated. There were points of my story, he said, that really connected. I gave thanks to the Lord, grateful my sharing had blessed him.

When we got to Monty's office, James introduced me to some of the other contractors. Several of these folks had heard of me. James' way of ministering to others always involves sharing a story or testimony. "This is Gene," he'd say as he introduced me, "you know ... the guy I told you about."

"Gene," Monty called out, motioning toward his office, "Come on in here. Let's chat." I noticed a manila folder in his hand as he closed the door behind us. I was thinking this was a job interview. He began though, saying, "You know, I'd love to offer you a job, but right now I don't have room to bring anyone else on." I was disappointed; this wasn't what I'd expected to hear. Before I could respond, though, Monty opened the folder and produced a check, saying, "The Holy Spirit told me to bring you back to the office and write you a check for $10,000."

Shock doesn't cut it—I was dumbstruck! I felt warm all over. Tingling, almost. And confused.

Is this for real? echoed in my head. I actually said those words out loud, too. You know that moment on reality television shows where someone points to a camera and tells you you've been pranked? Yeah. *Where's the camera?* I looked at the check and saw all those zeroes ... *Wow!* And the check was made out to *me*. Monty's eyes were teary above his ear-to-ear smile. I got teary, too. Tears of joy. His and mine.

A check for $10,000 was beyond my wildest imagination. But what Monty said next jolted me—it seemed to fulfill a prophetic vision I'd had years earlier in chapel. Monty said, "Welcome to Texas. Go buy yourself a car!"

Two years earlier, at Rockview, a group of about 50 guys gathered on Tuesday mornings for prayer. I always encouraged the guys to pray big and to be specific. I'd tell them: *Pray for when you get out of here, pray for a house, a car, a wife.* One of those Tuesdays I was praying through these big and specific things—a house, a car, a wife—with my friend and fellow lifer José. As we prayed, I began to thank God for hearing and answering our prayers, and I had a vision: I saw a silhouette of a man, reaching to hand me a set of car keys. I don't know how else to describe it other than saying that in that moment I felt a deep assurance God had heard my prayer. I told José about the experience, and I told him since God heard me about the car, I'd quit praying about that and just give Him thanks ... and pray harder about the house and a wife!

I told Monty that story. He gave thanks that he'd been obedient to the Lord's leading and that we'd both witnessed God's answer to my prayer. It was a tremendously worshipful experience, a sacred moment—right there in a roofing contractor's office.

Driving away with James that day, I walked back through what had just happened. I told him how I felt when Monty produced the check, about our interaction, about the sharp recollection of my prayer with José. James and I rejoiced together. Another worshipful experience. I told James I had hoped Monty might offer me a job. James assured me, "God's got other plans."

I had been borrowing Larry's car while he and Devi were out of the country.

I'd dropped it in a parking lot so that James and I could ride together to lunch, so he took me back to retrieve it. I reached into one pocket for the car keys, and re-checked the other—*Yes, the check is still there!*

After James pulled away, I sat there for several more minutes, still in awe of God's goodness. I thought through the months of depending on others for rides ... how I'd talked to Larry about borrowing money to buy a car—which he counseled me *not* to do, but rather to wait on the Lord. God is so good!

I put the car in reverse and started rolling backward, slowly. *CRUNCH!* I'd just experienced another first: my first car accident.

I got out to take a look. There was a pretty good-sized dent in this lady's rear fender. I was nervous. I had no idea what to do. I'd only had my license three days. I didn't have any insurance.

"What were you thinking?" the lady asked. "Didn't you see me?"

I hadn't seen her. I apologized. I quickly dialed James—*he couldn't have gotten too far*. I said, "Hey, I just backed into this lady."

He teased, "Don't worry! I've been through this a few times ... with my kids!"

While we waited for James to return, I stood next to the lady's car, chatting with her as she leaned back in her seat. I couldn't help but notice her car was absolutely filled with stuff, hoarder-like. She told me things had been tough as of late. She'd been out of work for a while, disabled. I asked her if I could pray for her. We were praying when James pulled up. He may have gotten a few more beginner-driver teases in, but he helped us sort out all the information we'd need to get this taken care of. I was relieved.

That night, Larry called to check in. I told him about the accident, and that I'd put a little crease in his fender. I also told him about Monty's generous gift and the answer to prayer. Larry responded, "Well it's unfortunate that you had the accident, Gene. But on the other hand, good that God provided you the resources to pay for the damage." Touché.

A few days later, I headed to Pennsylvania. I'd been invited to speak at seven different churches over 10 days. At each of these events, I was overwhelmed to see God releasing people from anger, guilt and shame as I shared. Most of the questions people asked centered around how I was not bitter about my circumstances. I could only explain my feelings: my sin against God was far greater than any sin against me. *Who was I not to forgive?*

God is love. He keeps no record of wrongs, no ledger of past offenses to hold over our heads. Like the father in the prodigal son parable in the Bible, our Heavenly Father stands waiting with open arms, not a boney finger of judgment to point out all our transgressions. His forgiveness is freeing. Unshackling. Welcoming. He says, "Come!"

In much the same way, our forgiveness of others is freeing—it frees us from harboring bitterness and hurt. But this is a tough lesson to learn, and even harder to apply. I marveled on my way back to Texas, after those speaking engagements, that God would bring this liberating message to others *through my story.*

For James, work was steady and growing. He asked me to come work for him, but not in a traditional roofer role. He said, "Gene, I need to travel to meet customers and visit jobsites and suppliers. I hate being on the road alone. You could come with me, help out and generally minister to those we meet. What do you think?" I loved the idea. Especially if it meant I wouldn't be climbing too many ladders!

I enjoyed being on the road with James. We'd work through the week and head back home for the weekends. Our first job in Oklahoma City was to repair a flat roof on a Christian school. The roof's rubber surface was beat to shards by sharp-edged hail, compromising the building's interior. The extensive water damage from all the melting ice and rain was devastating to see. Ceiling panels had disintegrated and caved in on the floors and furnishings of the sanctuary, classrooms and nursery.

As James specked out the jobs and provided direction and oversight to his crews, I met the people whose homes, businesses and churches we were repairing. It was such a blessing for me to hear their hearts—to just listen. And James recognized these dear people were hurting. He wanted to help heal their pain along the way to repairing their roofs. That was the role he'd envisioned for me.

James' crew at work was something to see. These men would put up a 15-foot ladder and run up it hands-free, carrying a bundle of shingles on each shoulder. James had me carry a couple bundles of shingles up myself—I think this was just so he could watch me do it and chuckle. I don't hold that against him; I must have been a comical sight! My lifelong fear of heights combined with worries about 60 pounds of shingles falling on my head ... let's just say I'm not a natural-born roofer. I rather like having my feet on solid ground. But I gained profound respect for the brave and skilled folks who do this every day.

One day, James and I stood looking up at the finial atop the biggest Methodist church in the city. The spire's storm-damaged copper wrap needed to be replaced. James probably saw the apprehension in me ... *That sure is way up there!*

"We will handle this job ourselves," he commented. I heard him say it ... and hoped he was joking.

The next thing I knew, he had pulled out his phone and was ordering a 100-foot basket lift. *He's serious! Could I quit on the spot?*

There was already a 60-foot lift onsite. "Come on," he said. "Let's see how close we can get with this." James seemed a little rusty on operating this lift, which didn't inspire a lot of confidence in me—it only increased my anxiety.

"You use these often?" I asked nervously.

The ride up was down-right hairy! The wind was whipping, the basket was swaying back and forth, the herky-jerkyness of it all—I was terrified! I swear, I was trying to dig my toes through my work boots and straight into the lift's metal floor. I was certain with every movement we were about to topple over. I gripped the handrails so tightly my fingers burned. The lift reached its limit, and we were still several feet short of the finial. Realizing we'd come up short, James maneuvered us down. I praised God all the way back to earth. "No worries," he said, "we'll have the 100-footer here tomorrow." *Oh joy!*

As promised and nervously anticipated, the next morning up we went. The wind was blowing pretty good, and things on the ground were looking awfully small as we rose. Somewhere around 80 feet I quit looking down. I told myself to just focus straight ahead. I kept telling James to move the basket closer to the steeple, the further we went up. I was probably a subconscious plea hoping for somewhere I could latch onto for dear life ... you know, until firefighters could get there to rescue me.

When we reached the very top, the basket stopped rising. But it didn't stop swaying side-to-side. We wobbled like that the whole time, and we had to reach way out to lift the 10-foot long, 60-pound, copper-covered, hail-pelted finial and post off its perch and settle it into our basket-lift. I held my breath. Finally, at long last, we had the piece we'd come for aboard and secured, and we began our decent. *Hallelujah! Thank You, Jesus!*

Our trip across town to the metal supply shop gave me time to recover. On the way, James said, "Gene, I've got to take you in to meet Big John and share your testimony." Big John owned the business, and if ever a man lived up to his nickname, it was him: John is a *big* man, and he met us with a big smile and big, warm greeting when we arrived.

"Pleasure to meet you," he said, extending his big hand. "Have a seat!" We moved through introductions and pleasantries and I was given the opportunity to share how faithful God had been in redeeming and restoring my life. Tears filled Big John's eyes as I spoke.

Then he shared with us that his sister had died five years earlier—that he'd been angry and filled with grief over the loss. It wasn't fair. She was too young. He said that hearing my story, and particularly that I'd not given up serving God in spite of all the years I'd been incarcerated, convicted him—he wanted to receive God's healing and restoration in his life. He wanted to be free of the anger and bitterness. We cried and prayed together.

A week later, James and I had occasion to visit Big John again. The change in him was palpable—he was a changed man, a new man, freed from his burden.

Working with James was filled with these sorts of experiences—like divine encounters. At another job site, we bumped into a homeless man pushing a shopping cart full of items he'd collected from dumpsters. We had a wonderful conversation, helped him out with a little bit of money and prayed together. And I learned this was James' pattern; everywhere he goes, he's sensitive to the Lord's leading and divine appointments. I grew accustomed to seeing James open his heart—and his wallet—to people in need.

And the finial? I have to tell you, for some strange reason I looked forward to our putting the shiny, newly copper-wrapped piece back in its place. Like a gut check—*Gotta do this!* I still didn't look down. But it felt awesome to set it back on its mount ... and to descend right after. It looked great. From the ground.

Thoughts of having a place of my own, my very own apartment, started just a few months after my release. Don't get me wrong, I was blessed to have stayed with Larry and Devi in their beautiful Colleyville home for my first few months in Texas, and then to have James and Trina invite me to move into the two-room mother-in-law suite attached to their home. I accepted, offering to pay a few hundred bucks a month in rent—which James resisted at first—but I convinced him it would help me work on budgeting and expenses and give me a taste of what being on my own would require. I was aiming to be on my own two feet sooner rather than later.

The Lozanos' mother-in-law suite was fully furnished. And fully outfitted. I really didn't need to buy anything for myself other than groceries. And *that* was an experience in itself—shopping. My first trip to the grocery store for myself was a little stressful. I get this big shopping cart—*Texas big*, mind you—and steer it up and down all these wide aisles. And choices? The cereal aisle alone I must have walked three times. *Why are there so many different kinds of cereal? Are they really all different?* In prison we had two: Corn Flakes and Cheerios. (There was this one time when they brought in some sugar-coated cereal, Frosted Flakes maybe, but it was short-lived. A couple of the knuckleheads got into a fight over the last bowl of the sugared stuff. We never saw it again.)

This will sound funny, but it was sort of an emotional experience for me. I pulled out my cell phone and, as inconspicuously as possible, snapped a photo down the aisle. I texted the picture to my friend Patty with the caption, "So many choices!"

She wrote back, "Welcome to freedom!"

The idea of having a little autonomy when it came to my living conditions excited me. I'd been a kid, supported by my parents for 17 years, then I became a *guest* of the State of Pennsylvania for the next 35. A year, then, being nurtured by the kindness and hospitality of the Tituses and Lozanos, I was really feeling eager to stand on my own two feet and take care of myself.

I dreamed of owning a home. But I recognized that as a longer-term goal. A good start would be an apartment. I was pretty confident I could meet the obligations, cover the rental expenses and manage this on my own. It was time to step out in faith.

Thoughts of how to arrange a place of my own, with furniture, pictures, color schemes of towels and kitchen items—it was all exciting. And to control the television remote! I'd never had autonomy like that.

At Rockview, I'd earned *single-cell status* due to my seniority and because I'd maintained a stellar prison record. But in times of overcrowding, I would have to share my cell with another inmate. Whenever that happened, I always viewed the space as equally ours, not mine. Some inmates were just the opposite—you'd hear about possessive guys dividing their 9x7 cell into sections, telling the new guy, "This is yours" and "This is mine!" Ridiculous stuff, too, like making up rules about where the new guy could sit or stand, when he could use the toilet. I wanted to be a servant, like Jesus—

"And consider the example that Jesus, the Anointed One, has set before us. Let his mindset become your motivation. He existed in the form of God, yet he gave no thought of seizing equality with God as his supreme prize. Instead he emptied himself of his outward glory by reducing himself to the form of a lowly servant" (Philippians 2:5-7 TPT).

Adopting this mindset is hard. It's really hard. The more I've studied it, the more I've realized that servants have no rights. No entitlements. Servants consider others more important than themselves—put others' needs before their own. If it wasn't enough for me reading it in Scripture, it's probably the one message Larry spoke into my life more than any other over all those years. But in those times when you know you're being stepped on, taken advantage of, manipulated ... holding on to the desire *I want to be like Jesus* is not easy.

There were times when I literally put my face to the concrete cell floor and prayed, *I have been crucified with Christ; it is no longer I who live but Christ who lives in me; and the life which I now live in the flesh I live by faith in the Son of God, who loved me and gave Himself for me. I can do all things through Christ who gives me strength. Jesus, live through me and make me a servant.* That prayer changed my life and changed how I would impact the guys around me in the prison, for the Kingdom.

Finding an apartment was a bit of a challenge. Somewhere in the dialogue with potential landlords, or in the application process, I had to reveal the fact that I'm a convicted felon. In some cases, it was a deal-breaker before there was even a deal on the table. A few people were kind, listening to my story. "You can Google it," I'd tell them.

But you get used to hearing, "I'm sorry." It hurts to be rejected. Summarily dismissed. I'd think, *It was 35 years ago!* and *I'm going to be a great tenant!* No matter. It's hard not to become discouraged.

There were a few lighter-hearted experiences, too. I looked at a few sketchy places where, when the landlord said *No*, I was like, *Thank You, Jesus!*

I'd go back and talk to James after each attempt, and he would ask, "Why do you want to move out? You know you're welcome here." It wasn't as if anything specific was prompting me to want out. I worked with James. Went to church with James. We were always together. And he and Trina have *their* life. They never made me feel like I was a burden, but I surely didn't want to become one. It was just time.

Then the Lord opened a door. I toured the Copper Hill Apartments property. Kathy, the apartment manager, showed me around. She knew about my record but felt like my application would go through. She offered to pray with me before I left. *Wow!* It was perfect for me. The apartment even had a little concrete patio where I could sit with my morning coffee, pray and read. I tried not to get my hopes up too high, you know?

Kathy called me the next day; my application was accepted! I signed a one-year lease. And then the excitement really kicked in. The sting of all the rejections, one after another, faded away. I had a place of my own, just a few miles away in Bedford.

I raced back to tell James and Trina the good news. On the drive, I thought about Henry and Big Moses. *If they could see me now!* They'd be so happy for me. I couldn't wait for the next time one of them called me, so I could share the news.

Then it hit me: this was *my* apartment—my *completely empty* apartment. I had nothing. No bed. No furniture. No towels. No plates to eat off. No silverware to eat with. Autonomy wasn't so attractive in this moment of gravitas; I'd gone from *Unshackled* ... to *unfurnished*!

Trina had my back. "Don't you worry, Gene. I've got extra dishes, pots and pans. We even have an extra bed with a brand-new mattress you can take. And other people will help, too." There I was thinking autonomy, and God was using this to experience to remind me of the blessing of community. Trina's friend Claire guided me from Grapevine to Fort Worth searching consignment shops for bargains. In no time at all, I had living room furniture and a bedroom set, with all my *new* stuff staged in James' garage waiting for move-in day.

Then, the day arrived! I didn't have much—we loaded up James' truck, and a short time later I was settling in. That moment, though, when the last of the helpers left and I turned the deadbolt behind them and sat down—*Ah!* Alone. *My first apartment.* I was emotional. I felt so blessed. But also a little strange. I'd never been alone like this before. There was always *someone* else around. Shared space. Being alone was quiet. Really quiet.

My mind drifted back to the cell blocks at Rockview where there was always a constant flow of noise; guys shouting from one cell to the next, a basketball game on a television, radios playing different stations up and down the range. Clamorous, every waking hour.

Quiet and stillness like this was a little unsettling for me at first. It would take some getting used to.

Things got better with the morning. I'm a breakfast guy. Eggs, coffee, toast—Trina had given me a toaster. I made my breakfast. In my place. This felt good. And I was excited to get my day in gear—there were a few errands I needed to run, tasks I needed to complete. I had to order my day, the very same process of life that everyone goes through. I know it may not sound like a big deal, but when you've spent so many years—my entire adult life—with other people ordering your days for you, it really is something to plan your own day.

I kept my eyes open for opportunities to meet and interact with my new neighbors. It wasn't a really social complex; everybody was on the go. So was I. I was off chasing storms with James. In fact, those first few months, I was rarely in my apartment. I was grateful for my job and enjoyed working with James, but I was starting to feel ready for another life-change.

The Snooty Pig Café—I smiled at the name as I walked in to meet Larry one morning for breakfast. We started by catching up over some funny stories. He told me about a well-known pastor friend of his who was speaking during a prayer service, and a man with one leg was in the front row. The pastor looked over and said, "Well, hop on over here so I can pray for you, friend!" Larry's laughter reminded me of how joyful he is about life, no matter the circumstances.

Having a sage-like father figure in your life is a marvelous thing. So many men struggle in their lives. Having someone who will listen to you from the heart and offer you astute observations and insights to consider is priceless. Looking back over my relationship with Larry, he had been such a constant for me; his wisdom helped me learn how to hear clearly from the Holy Spirit. I owe Larry a debt of gratitude I will never be able to repay.

My purpose in meeting with Larry this morning was two-fold: I wanted to catch up, but I also wanted to apologize to him. I started with the apology.

"I am sorry about the distance I've created between us this past year," I said. "You have been faithful to me, and I want to ask your forgiveness."

"Absolutely!" he said. Tears welled up in our eyes. There was a moment of silence across the table.

"How have we offended you?" Larry asked. Those words stirred up what was hidden beneath the surface. I wasn't sure any of it really needed revisiting, but we did need to clear the air to some extent. It is the loving thing to do.

I explained how, when I was first released, he and Devi indicated they'd raise a salary for me, which they did in part. I hadn't understood, going in, that they expected me to raise part of my salary by reaching out to friends and family for support. I wasn't aware they'd be sending out a support letter on my behalf until the day they handed it to me and asked me to sign it. I had never asked anyone for any support during my time in prison. The letter bothered me. I was embarrassed, pleading for others to support *my* ministry. I recognize that donor support is how vital ministries like KGM are able to function, and how missionaries are supported on the field. It just wasn't what I, myself, had expected ... and being honest with Larry, now, I wasn't comfortable with the arrangement.

When you love people, miscommunications and misunderstandings happen. It was a very good thing that we could share openly with each other and really listen to one another. God is a God of forgiveness and healing. We, as His children, are too. It's our new nature. And the Bible paints a beautiful picture in Psalm 133 (NIV)—

"How good and pleasant it is when God's people live together in unity! It is like precious oil poured on the head, running down on the beard, running down on Aaron's beard, down on the collar of his robe. It is as if the dew of Hermon were falling on Mount Zion. For there the LORD bestows his blessing, even life forevermore."

Everything was going pretty well. I was getting more requests to share my story, in Texas, back in Pennsylvania and new opportunities around the country. David Diaz, who pastors New Beginnings Church in Baldwin Park, CA, invited me to speak at an event—it would be my first trip to the West Coast. They'd arranged two rooms for us at the Hilton—Fernando, a worship leader from Larry's church, traveled with me; he would lead the gathering in song, and then

I'd speak. We arrived on Saturday for the Sunday service.

Checked in and settled, we decided to take advantage of the hotel's hot tub. Fernando got down there before me; he was bubbling like a lobster in a pot when I walked in. I had never been in a hot tub before, but it looked pretty amazing ... and inviting. The smell of chorine, the stirring waters, the heat rising, God's goodness overwhelmed me—here I was, three months out of Rockview, and across the country in LA, climbing into a hot tub and ...

My very first step, I lost my footing. Slipped right out from under me. Sort of like if you live up North and slip on the ice—my foot went flying. My mind kicked into warp speed, telling me *You're going down, hard.* There's that split second where every muscle in your body tenses, hoping against hope to stop the fall, or break the fall. To no avail. I grabbed for a handrail; the very same handrail I watched my knee slam into, causing the sharpest pain I'd ever experienced. I screamed in agony. I still had no footing and no grip—I went down on my back, a blast of water hit my face. I reached for my knee, instinctively.

Then I saw Fernando's face ... he was mortified at what he saw.

I looked down at my knee and it looked broken. You could see a bone protruding up against the skin where my kneecap should have been. I cried out for Fernando to go get help. He suggested, "Pop it back into place."

I pleaded, "Please get help!" He shot out of that water and raced for the lobby.

I gripped my knee with both hands. I put pressure on my kneecap and tried to flex and bend the joint. It produced pain like I'd never experienced, radiating up and down my entire leg. Then, all of a sudden, it popped back into place. The pain greatly relieved—maybe a 10 down to a 5 or so—I sat and waited for Fernando to return with help.

I felt stupid; all those years of being athletic, playing pretty rugged prison-yard sports with virtually no protective equipment ... and I'd never been injured *then*. Now? I'm stepping into a bath, and ... *this?!*

Right before my eyes, my knee swelled quickly to twice its normal size. Fernando returned; paramedics were on the way. Perfect.

At the ER, waiting to be X-rayed, Fernando placed a call to Larry and Devi to fill them in. I overheard Fernando saying to Devi, "No, Ma'am. We weren't horse playing! Gene just slipped." Yes, it's really that lame a story.

They gave me some pain meds and an immobilizer for my knee. "You'll need to see an orthopedist when you get back to Texas," the doctor told me. An orthopedist? I didn't even have a primary care doctor. And I didn't have any medical insurance. *What had I just done?*

The pastors of the church where I was to speak walked in. They offered to cancel the service and send me home. I told them, "No. I want to do this. I can do it on crutches. We pray up and we press forward." So that's what we did.

It wasn't until the flight home that it all really started to dawn on me: things just got really complicated really fast. *How was I going to be able to work? How was I going to pay for this orthopedist? How would I keep up with my bills?*

All of this, and *I never even got to enjoy the hot tub.*

CHAPTER 4

LOOKING UP

Back home, sitting in my apartment with my leg propped up, I took a deep breath and sighed. Trying to imagine what was next, I had more questions than answers. I was reminded of something I'd heard Larry say many times over the years: "Being flat on your back isn't a bad place to be, especially when your only view is looking up."

Texas Orthopedics' office was just a few miles from my apartment. Driving myself to my appointment was quite an adventure. My right leg was fixed in an immobilizer, so just getting into the car was stressful and physically challenging. Adjusting the driver's seat all the way back and lifting the bad leg in, sliding it up under the dashboard as far as I could, trying to fold the rest of my body in and down onto the seat—I worked up quite a sweat. I must have been a sight. It's hard to even describe the contortion it took to get into position to drive. I drove very slowly and deliberately, just about the entire time trying to imagine how I was going to get myself up and out of the car when I arrived.

I had no idea as to the extent of my injury before Dr. Harris walked in. He was wearing a white coat and a big, friendly smile. "What did you do, Mr. McGuire?" I told him I slipped and fell entering a hot tub. He teased, "You might want to come up with a better story!"

He began examining my leg. "Flex your thigh muscle for me." I did as he said. "So, you can't flex it?" he asked.

"I just did," I answered.

He gave me a pity-filled smile ... "No, you can't flex it. It never moved." I was stunned. It absolutely felt to me like I'd tightened that muscle, just as he directed.

"I'm pretty confident you've ruptured your patella tendon. You may have a complete tear, but we will need an MRI to confirm this before we go any further." He scribbled some notes and started the process of getting me to radiology for imaging. "You've done quite a number on that knee," he said. "This is one of the more serious knee injuries to have."

This is so crazy. Throughout my incarceration, I had been in several extremely tough predicaments, but nothing made me feel as uncomfortable as the crumpling of the white paper beneath me on the exam table—it might as well have been *butcher paper.* The seriousness of his tone and the way he spoke so directly made me wonder if this would be a lifelong injury. I felt nervous, scared, alone. In other situations that were stressful, I'd think, *Gene, fix your eyes on Jesus, the Author and Finisher of your faith.* I knew I needed to do that here ... and I know God is faithful—but the struggle was real.

Throughout my most difficult times in prison, the Lord always offered Himself as the solution for me, even before His provision came through, so that I would know Him *better.* This was my assurance to fall back on as I sat in that exam room: *I knew the Lord had a plan for this, even though I couldn't see it.*

Dr. Harris asked, "Why did you wait so long to see a doctor?" I explained that I was hoping it would get better. And since I didn't have insurance, I didn't really know who to turn to for help.

"A friend of mine told me you did her shoulder surgery," I said. "She recommended I come see you."

I also confessed to him that I felt pretty stupid. All those years I'd spent participating in prison sports—12 years of tackle football, 25 years of softball, seven years of power-lifting—and now this? *I slipped stepping into a hot tub? I destroyed my knee ... in a hot tub?*

"So how bad is it?" I finally asked.

His answer was point-blank: "You need emergency surgery. You really needed it the day this happened. If you don't get it soon, you could lose the use of your leg." I was trying to block out that last part. "You've waited 17 days. It's amazing you're not in more pain than you are. But I can't get a slot in the OR until Tuesday, so you will have to wait a few more days."

Then he laid out the cost for me. He would need to charge me a few hundred dollars for the MRI and around $1,500 for the surgery. He said the hospital would charge me somewhere around $20,000. All of those numbers sounded astronomical and impossible to me—I just didn't have it.

"Tell me again how this happened," he prompted.

"I was in LA to share a testimony of God's faithfulness in my life over the 35 years I was in prison. And I slipped getting into the hotel hot tub the night before."

He then asked me to tell him a little of my story, so I gave him a quick summary: crime, life sentence, prison life, coming to faith, God's faithfulness.

Dr. Harris excused himself for a moment. He returned with two associates to examine my knee and asked me to share my story again, with them. In that moment, I felt like I was exactly where God wanted me to be. I was in the best place for me to be. I was in God's *pleasing and perfect will* like it says in Romans 12.

I told Dr. Harris that I didn't have any insurance. "I have $2,200 in my bank account. I can give you $1,000 today," I said, "and I'll raise some more money somehow ..."

He stopped me. "Hold on a moment." He stepped out again, this time returning with a young female assistant.

"Listen. My assistant Kirsten is going to get some more information from you. You are in good hands with her. Then, before you leave this room, call this number." He handed me a card. "This lady works at the Harris Methodist Hospital in Southlake, and she assists people who don't have insurance. She is expecting your call. You make the call, and Kirsten will arrange for you to have the surgery Tuesday."

I had no idea what was happening, but I was overjoyed and elated. A wave of relief washed over me. I felt God's peace—the kind that says, and reassures, *You will get through this.*

I teared up. Then those tears flowed. All I could say was, "Thank you! Thank you so much!!"

Moments later I was dialing the number to speak with one of the administrators at Harris Methodist. She took down my financial information and told me she'd be requesting financial assistance for me from the president of the hospital. Again, fighting back tears, "Thank you! Thank you!"

Back home, leg propped, deep breath and sigh ... Larry was right: *Flat on your back isn't a bad place to be.* I stretched my hands out and worshiped the Lord. I mimicked Jehoshaphat in 2 Chronicles 20, when, facing allied enemy armies, out-numbered and out-resourced, he resolved to *inquire of the Lord.* And in faith he proclaimed: "We will stand before this house and before you— for your name is in this house—and cry out to you in our affliction, and you will hear and save."

Lord, You saved me when I was dead in my sins; when Nookie and his buddies attacked me at Camp Hill with a padlock in a sock ... when I was surrounded in the prison chapel by men with clenched fists, ready to strike me ... when two fellow inmates confronted me with razor-knives on the cell-block ... when I was falsely accused of an assault against a C.O. and placed in the hole ... when I was sentenced to life without parole. I recall Your faithfulness and goodness to me then. Lord, help me now!

My phone rang. It was my friend Chris Baer.

"Gene! Hey, brother, would you be willing to share your testimony tomorrow at a restaurant in Decatur called Sweetie Pie's Ribeyes? I was telling the general manager, Mancha, about you, and he got permission from the owners, the Vinyard family, to have you come in, have lunch with their employees and speak.

Chris is one of the first guys I met here in Texas. I'd only been working for KGM a few days. I was sitting at the front desk, answering phone calls and greeting people. In walks this 6'5" model-looking guy, huge smile and a warm greeting: "You're Gene McGuire! I've heard all about you. It is a pleasure to meet you." Our conversation was long, winding ... and amazing. "Your story has to be told," he said.

Chris is a pastor. His ministry is in the marketplace. He'd been in church ministry before and was admittedly a little gun-shy of going back. I wanted to hear more. He invited me over for dinner and to meet his wife, Roni, and their children. It makes me smile even now to recall that visit—Chris actually tells the story best: "Honey, can I invite Gene McGuire over for supper? He was in prison for 35 years ... for murder ..."

When I got there, everyone just kept looking at me. It was funny then. It's funnier now, years later, for us all to reminisce.

Chris took time that evening to share his incredible testimony with me. One night, when he was eight years old and his sister, Kim, was four, they were playing outside. Their mom called them in for dinner, but Chris' sister never came. "About 15 minutes later," he said, "our next-door neighbor was banging on our door. When I opened it, he told us that my sister was trapped under our electric garage door. We all rushed out of the house to see her pinned and lifeless. My dad proceeded to give her CPR. I ran next door to get a neighbor who was a nurse. When I arrived back at the scene, my sister still had no pulse. She was dead. She had been without oxygen for over 15 minutes. A few minutes later, I witnessed what I now call a miracle; my sister started breathing and came back to life. Later that night, I looked up and said some words, not realizing it was my first prayer: 'I don't know who You are, but thank You.' Deep inside me, I knew there was a higher power, a superior being that did something remarkable right in front of my eyes. Four years later, the summer of 1982, I was introduced to that higher power. I heard the Gospel, and one night as I was laying on my bed His love overwhelmed me. I raised my hands to the heavens and started crying. I told Him that I understand and receive His love for me, that I want Him to be the Lord of my life. I asked Him to forgive me of my sins, and that night I invited that higher power into my heart and life forever—the Lord Jesus Christ."

Chris also walked me through more of the backstory on how he'd connected with the Vinyard family business. "I met Joel Vinyard at a Christian business get-together, and we were talking about business and chaplaincy." Chris had been ministering as a chaplain in his apartment complex, and that concept of ministry *outside of church* and *where people are* intrigued Joel. They went on to talk about the Vinyard family-owned restaurants, and Joel's desire that a chaplain could be on hand to minister to the spiritual needs of their managers and employees—real life people with real life concerns, needs and issues. Chris had been on the payroll several months now, serving two of their locations. The ministry was going very well, and Chris really enjoyed it.

I was captivated.

Chris and I started getting together twice a week after that, to grab coffee and a doughnut and talk.

"So, this invite," he clarified, "there won't be any honorarium. But Sweetie Pie's will provide lunch for us."

I was all in. "Absolutely," I said. "But you'll have to pick me up. I can't drive with this immobilizer on my knee."

When my scheduled speaking date arrived, walking into Sweetie Pie's was like going back in time. The place resembles life in the 1800s, with its western décor and old chairs and tables. I stopped to rest on my crutches and found myself face-to-face with this creature, stuffed and mounted on the wall.

A big, white-haired gentleman with a bushy moustache and heavy Texas drawl explained, "You're looking at a jackalope. These fellas were once fearsome critters on the prairies, and, interesting fact, their milk was known as a potent aphrodisiac." Then he extended his Texas-sized hand under a wide and welcoming smile. "I'm Joe Vinyard. My brother, Paul, is the owner. He just called and said he's running a few minutes late. But welcome!"

Some 40 employees were on hand. The mayor and a few local business owners were also invited. Chris opened the meeting with prayer; then he spoke briefly about his role as a chaplain for the restaurant and introduced me. I was really touched: *he called me his best friend*. At this point, I'd been in Texas about a year. I so appreciated Chris' presence in my life and our friendship.

As I shared my testimony, things got emotional. When I finished, I sat down in a chair, and Chris wrapped things up with an invitation for anyone who wanted to learn more about Jesus and a closing prayer. When he said "Amen," the man sitting next to me reached over and offered his hand. With tears in his eyes and in his very distinctive, deep baritone voice, he said, "Hey, bud, I'm Paul Vinyard. I am so glad to have you here this morning. It is a pleasure to meet you."

Paul explained that he had around 1,500 employees working in various locations throughout the Dallas-Fort Worth area. "I'd like them all to hear your testimony. If I can figure out how to do it, would you be willing?"

I explained that I was having surgery on Tuesday, so I was unsure of just how soon I'd be ready to do this, but *Yes!* I was very willing. I was thrilled and looking forward to the opportunity.

Back to my physical reality—I was facing surgery. I'd be out of work. My savings was dwindling. Rent was due in a couple of weeks. I called James and asked if I could stay with them after my surgery, just until I could get back on my feet. James said he'd talk it over with Trina—and called back to say it wouldn't be possible for them right now. I called my sister and asked her if I could make temporary arrangements to move back into her home in Pennsylvania while I recovered. She said she would talk to Joe about setting up for me, but to be honest, a hint of hesitation in Mary's voice concerned me. I really didn't want to be a burden to anyone.

Talking to my friend Patty, she volunteered to take a leave of absence from her job as a flight attendant, come to Texas and help me. She made plans to be with me through the surgery and to help me box up my things for storage or ship them to Pennsylvania ... whatever needed to happen. Patty was, and is, a godsend.

The night before my surgery, Larry stopped by to see me. He had a young Brazilian man named Ceilis with him. Ceilis, I'd guess, was in his late 20s. He had connected with Larry through KGM's ministry in Brazil and was here in the States for a visit. We talked for a while, and the fellowship really encouraged me. Larry prayed for me and my surgery.

"Don't get up!" Larry teased as he rose to head for the door. Just then, Ceilis said, "Hold up. I want to speak to Gene." Then turning to me, he said, "I have a word for you."

I was interested in what Ceilis had to share. I'd heard of things like this before—if God has a word, I certainly want to hear it!

"While we were praying," he said, "I saw Jesus standing in front of you with His hands stretched out to His sides. And He was telling you to sit there with your arms stretched out by your side and worship Him."

I was in tears by the time Ceilis finished, overwhelmed by God's goodness. I had been sitting *in this very chair* with my arms outstretched *just like that* praising God for two solid weeks!

Ceilis' words were a reminder and an encouragement: I was *in* God's perfect will! It had seemed like a brick wall stood in front of me—I had no idea what to do or where to go. But then, *one puzzle piece after another*, everything started falling into place.

My mind runs to the promise recorded in Romans 8:28: "And we know that in all things God works for the good of those who love him, who have been called according to his purpose."

His Divine providence continued to amaze me. Patty arrived from New Jersey and drove me to Methodist South Lake Hospital the next day. Checking in, they informed me that the president of the hospital had approved 100% coverage for my surgery. I was stunned! Almost in disbelief, I kept thinking, *Lord, what's going on? All this favor—I messed up my knee and had no idea how I'd get through this, and You have provided everything I've needed! Thank You!*

Surgery took a few hours. When I came out of recovery, Patty was right there, smiling like she had been when I went in. Dr. Harris came wearing his big smile and surgical scrubs; he said everything went very well. "I was amazed to find the tendon, which had torn off your kneecap, lying right there and hadn't rolled up into your thigh. There was very little dead tissue to cut away, even after 17 days with no blood flow. You are a blessed man."

Patty played around-the-clock nurse for me and did all the cleaning and shopping. She kept me laughing as the pain of having three holes drilled through my kneecap and the tendon tied off increased. There wasn't enough medication to ease the ache, but her friendship sure did.

While I was recovering at home my phone rang, and in that unmistakably deep voice and Texas drawl I heard, "Hey, bud, how's that leg doing?"

I told Paul that hurting it initially wasn't *this* painful! "Listen," he said, "I want to make sure you have enough food for the next couple of weeks, so I'd like to send, with your permission, one of my store managers over each night with meals from the restaurant." I was humbled—and grateful. What a blessing!

"I also want to fairly compensate you for speaking the other day. I'd like to give you $500 for your time, if you think that's fair." Once again, in awe and amazed: "Yes, sir! I think that is more than fair. Thank you."

"Also, if you're willing," he continued, "I have 11 other restaurants where we'd love for you to share your story with our employees on Saturday mornings. I'll pay you $500 for each one." I was thrilled at Paul's offer. I couldn't wait to call Mary and tell her not to worry—that the Lord had provided rent money so I could stay in my apartment in Texas.

Over the next two weeks, supervisors and general managers from Babe's, Bubba's and Sweetie Pie's came to my apartment and served Patty and I dinner. There was so much food every night—fried chicken, creamed corn, green beans caramelized in bacon fat and hot biscuits. Patty joked that her uniform wasn't going to fit when she went back to work.

One night, Bill, a supervisor of four of Babe's locations, called to say it was his turn to bring supper. He asked if I wanted something different. "You have to be getting tired of fried chicken. Have you ever had an Italian Beef? I know a place called Weinberger's Deli. They are from Chicago, where I'm from, and they have the best Italian Beef sandwiches in the world."

I told Bill that sounded great. So he responded, "Great! I'll pick up three of them and we'll eat at your place. See you soon!"

Once I became a little more self-sufficient, Patty headed home. I set my mind on rehab and getting my knee to bend again. It was a painful four months, walking on crutches and exercising to break up scar tissue. But I was making progress.

One Saturday I was scheduled to share my testimony at Babe's Granbury location. Paul and his wife, Charla, picked me up. During the ride, Paul told me of his concern for his employees. "Many of these young folks are dealing with personal issues and struggles. I am looking to hire a chaplain to come onboard and serve their needs. The job is yours, if you're interested."

The chaplain to a group of restaurants. Ministry in the marketplace. I loved the idea. "Yes! I'd love to serve as a chaplain!"

Arrangements were made. Chris had already begun serving two locations. I would start by visiting the Arlington store for a week, and then each week thereafter I'd add another location to my schedule. Pretty quickly, I settled into a routine: I kept up the discipline of spending time in my Bible at the start of each day as I did in prison. I'd spend time in prayer for the particular store I would visit each day, praying for the managers and employees by name. I prayed also for divine appointments, that God would have me *in just the right place at just the right time* to bless those I'd encounter. And, time after time, I would walk in the door and someone would inevitably say, "Gene! I am so glad you're here. Can I talk to you?" I would listen and love in Jesus' name.

At Babe's, I consider myself a resource; an extension of the God-honoring atmosphere and family-friendly culture our owners embody, and which permeates the entire establishment. Each day brings new opportunities.

A single mom overwhelmed with the responsibilities at home ... a student's anxiety over an upcoming exam ... someone's health concerns—I never know exactly what I'll encounter, but it is such an amazing privilege to listen to, pray with and encourage someone in Christ for a living.

And it's not your typical pastoral ministry environment—it's a restaurant full of guests, alive with the sounds of family gatherings, the smell of fried chicken and bacon fat, country music and line-dancing. Still, every prayer directed to God in faith is powerful. No heartfelt encouragement from God's Word ever returns void. It happens pretty often, too, that customers tell me they appreciated seeing prayer in the restaurant workplace setting. I'm conscious of the fact that *we* may be the only Bible some people ever read.

I especially love meeting new employees at their orientation meetings. I love to welcome them and reiterate how important *they* are to the Babe's organization. I take a moment to explain my role as a chaplain. I make it very clear: I am not a manager, so "I'm not your boss!" In fact, I work *for you*. I am here to serve *you* in any way I can.

With so many employees, the greatest challenge for me is getting to know everybody and building relationships. Since relationships have an eternal value, they are far more important than our projects. This is what first impressed me about Paul Vinyard, who told me when we met, "God gave me a chicken business in order to raise up young people to become leaders." He also shared his passion for maintaining a down-to-earth, family-owned restaurant company, avoiding the ivory tower concept that creates an environment where owners are cut off from employees. "We don't have corporate offices," he said. "Our offices are located in our homes or in the front seat of one of the Ford F250 pickup trucks we provide for our supervisors."

Ownership and management's commitment to the golden rule is palpable. And you see the fruit of this calling everywhere you look.

One example is Scott Avery. I met Scott one hot summer's day on a par-3 golf course. His larger-than-life and boisterous personality match his frame; he's intimidatingly large—a former Northern Arizona University lineman—but a gentle giant.

Scott expressed an interest in restaurants, so I put him in touch with one of our supervisors. The rest, as they say, is history. Over the course of six years, Scott has become the general manager at Carrollton. He's like my Texas version of Big Moses: I get early morning calls from Scott, shouting, "Hey, brother! Wake up and praise the Lord! It's time to put those feet of yours on the floor and get this day started!" Everyone needs a Scott Avery in their life.

I was headed west along Loop 12 ... a man on a mission. It was a beautiful day out, work was done, and I had plans to work out in the late afternoon sun and jump in the pool for a swim. The prompting came out of nowhere: *Run by the Frisco location*.

It didn't make sense, as I had just been to the Frisco store the day before. I wasn't aware of any pressing concern. Nevertheless, I offered up a quick prayer like, *If this is You, Lord, let me be a blessing to someone there this afternoon*. I turned right onto the tollway, headed north.

On the way, I thought about how distinct His voice can be, and how often it takes us weeks or even months to hear Him because we either don't want to hear Him or we haven't taken the time to really listen. I wasn't going to miss this opportunity. I'll admit, though, I did think about how nice that pool would have felt on such a hot summer day.

Pulling into Babe's, I felt a real sense of purpose. Divine purpose. Although I had no idea just what it was. I sat for a moment in the parking lot and quoted Luke 4:18, as I often do: "The Spirit of the Lord is on me and has anointed me to proclaim good news to the poor; He has sent me to proclaim liberty to the captives and recovering of sight to the blind, to set at liberty those who are oppressed."

The general manager greeted me with a hug as I came in the door. "Gene? What are you doing here again?"

Not sure how to explain my change of plans, I explained that I was just driving and ... felt like stopping back.

"Glad you're here," he said, excusing himself to return to his tasks.

The dining room was full. The staff was busy. Country music played loud from the old-style jukebox, and the chatter of a packed house made it feel like a holiday. I noticed one of the servers, a college student named Candace, walk by. The Holy Spirit said, "Ask her if you can pray for her wrist."

I noticed a large brace wrapped around her wrist and hand as she carried a large serving tray—a big platter of fried chicken, piled high, with all the fixings—maneuvering across the dining room to her table. On her way back, I said, "Hey, Candace, what happened?" She explained that it was a lingering injury from her college days of tumbling and cheerleading. I could see she was in a lot of discomfort. "Can I pray for you? Pray that God heals this injury?"

I should say, it is a particular privilege to pray for people in this right-where-they-are fashion. It's not always possible; sometimes circumstances prohibit it. These dear people are at work and have customers to serve, and sometimes people just aren't comfortable praying right out in the open. I always try to be sensitive to both. In this instance, Candace smiled and welcomed my prayer, right on the spot.

A few minutes later, another young server walked by wearing a similar support brace on her wrist. I thought, *Okay, Lord, I'm sensing a pattern here.* I offered to pray for her when she was free. I spent the rest of my visit watching and listening, seizing every opportunity to offer prayer and encouragement.

Someone once asked me over coffee to share my five-year plan with them. I didn't need to. I explained that while I have some long-term dreams, since I've become a Christian I've learned to seek God's will for my life through my daily devotions in the Word and prayer. I desire to do *His* will. I rarely get the big picture in advance or even the blueprints of where life is going or what God is doing behind the scenes. It is my responsibility to present myself, saying "Here I am, Lord." I memorized Romans 12:1-2 very early in my Christian walk—

"I appeal to you therefore, brothers, by the mercies of God, to present your bodies as a living sacrifice, holy and acceptable to God, which is your spiritual worship. Do not be conformed to this world, but be transformed by the renewal of your mind, that by testing you may discern what is the will of God, what is good and acceptable and perfect."

It felt good that I was able to partner with God in His divine purposes that afternoon, to accomplish His good, acceptable and perfect will. It was better than a summer afternoon swim.

Often as I make the 45-mile drive north to Frisco, with worship music blaring—*Way Maker* or *Song of Deliverance* comes on, and I sort of lose myself in gratitude and amazement, thinking, *If my friends could see me now.*

For just a moment, it is like the music grows quiet, buildings and structures I'm passing fade into a blur, and I flashback—

Me and the guys, confined to 7x9 cells, on a 30-acre compound, surrounded by 20-foot razor-wired fencing, served up steaming plates of, say, *Seafood Newburg*—at least that's what they called the menu-staple, pungent-smelling noodle casserole. "There's fish in there," they'd say. *Sure ...*

Having spent three-quarters of my life incarcerated, I have so many memories of time with the guys that will never fade away. Nor would I want them to. Warner, Orlando, Henry, Hammer, Surf, Raffy, Louie, Scott—these guys are family. These recollections are family memories. We share one another's burdens, and we celebrate one another's successes.

The greatest character lessons I've experienced over the years I learned living in prison with these guys—*as iron sharpens iron.* That's a great analogy, actually: like metal being forged, heat applied and hammer stuck. Spending quality time in the Word and in prayer, learning to love and serve others in a most challenging environment to do just that—those weren't wasted years for any of us.

———

The waiting room on the fourth floor of the hospital resembled a Sunday morning at Waterside Church. Just about the entire congregation had turned out to pray for one of their members, Chris. We were all in shock at the news.

He was extremely fit, vibrant—coaching a high school football game just a couple nights prior ... *and now*? He hadn't felt well, was admitted to the hospital, diagnosed with viral meningitis and encephalitis and placed on a respirator—all within 24 hours. Doctors told Chris' wife, Cheryl, to notify family because, "It won't be long now."

Chairs in the waiting room had been reconfigured as people grouped up to pray and console one another. The sight of Cheryl having to be dressed in a surgical mask and gown to enter the room to be with her husband ripped at my heart.

Chris' parents and family flew in from Indiana. Chris' friend Jason and I volunteered to meet them at the airport and shuttle them to the hospital. Seeing the hurt in their faces, the shock, the disbelief ... I prayed in desperation, "Lord, help them! Lord, help us all!"

Chris' sister had so many questions in the car. "Just tell me everything you don't want to tell me," she insisted. We shared all we knew: doctors had told Cheryl Chris was struggling, and to expect with each passing hour things would worsen ... that there wasn't anything more they could do. *He's in a coma. He's on a respirator. That's all we know.* She rode in silence the rest of the way.

Family rushed in to see Chris as soon as we arrived. Pastor Chris Baer had organized a men's prayer group for 7 p.m. in the lobby. Two dozen men gathered to pray. One of the church's elders, John, opened the prayer time with the words "Yahweh Shamma," which means *God-who-is-here* in a way that reminded us all that although Chris' parents had arrived, Chris' Heavenly Father was here, too. We prayed that we would all feel and sense His presence; and especially that Chris—in this desperate hour—was experiencing the power of God's presence.

Men took turns praying around the room, each agreeing with one another—many adding an emphatic *Amen* or *Hallelujah*. I felt God's presence tangibly. I gave thanks: "Lord, we have everything we need here for a miracle tonight."

Once the prayer meeting over, a few of us ventured back up to the crowded waiting room. People had brought in food and drinks and some large containers of coffee. I snapped a couple pictures on my iPhone, thinking Chris would love to see all of support when he recovered.

Another day passed. Doctors told Cheryl there were no changes in his condition—he hadn't improved, *but* he hadn't gotten any worse. We all continued to pray. Pastor Chris prayed boldly, praying for Chris to rise up, that the enemy would not lay claim to this man of God. Everyone agreed in chorus, adding a hearty "Amen!"

Jason and I were talking. Neither of us could believe we were here. We had just traveled two hours to watch Chris coach a playoff game the night before all this began. "You want to go back to see Chris with me?" he asked. Absolutely, I did! We gowned up and masked up to enter the ICU.

The first thing that caught my attention entering the room was the respirator. Chris lay still on the bed; his chest rising and falling with the machine. "He's been just like this for three days," Jason said.

Jason stood on one side of the bed, and I was on the other. We prayed over our friend. Jason prayed, "Father, you brought Chris too far to leave him in this condition." I agreed in my spirit from the bottom of my heart. I'd known Chris to have gone through a real transformation in his life and in his marriage—God was really at work.

Jason began speaking to Chris. "Hey, buddy! If you can hear me, open your eyes." He repeated, "Can you hear me, Chris? Open your eyes for me." A few seconds later, again. I could hear the desperation in Jason's voice. I felt it, too. All of a sudden, Chris' eyes seemed to move beneath the lids. Jason and I both saw it, and then looked stunned at one another, like, *Tell me you saw that!*

"Chris," Jason said again, "open your eyes if you can hear me." And with that, Chris' eyes popped open for a split second and shut.

"Talk to him, Jason," I said. "He hears you!" Jason spoke more, Chris' eyes flickered. He groaned a little. Every hair on my body stood straight on end. Jason ran out of the room to collect Cheryl and family—they all raced in.

For the next several hours, we continued to pray. We started to get updates—Chris was improving, starting to wake up and be cognizant. We prayed on! The waiting room was ecstatic; people praying were filled with joy! Word came that they'd taken Chris off the respirator; he was talking and smiling and had asked for something to eat. Praise the Lord!

We'd witnessed a miracle. It occurred to me that I had just spoken at Waterside Church the week before on miracles … not expecting that in *one week's time* we'd all have an example. But this was something: The doctors had said, "Gather family … there's nothing more we can do" … and you see the tubes and wires, and you hear the respirator and see the monitors, and you pray … not knowing. Hoping. Waiting.

Our celebration continued the next Sunday at Waterside. Chris worshipped with us.

CHAPTER 5

UNSHACKLED

"You really need to write a book."

Since the day we'd met, Chris made a point of saying this to me almost every time we got together. And people everywhere I'd had the privilege of sharing my story with seemed to agree. I wasn't so sure. I had a few significant concerns.

First and foremost, my story begins with someone's murder. And not just someone—to her family members and friends, and the people of Lake Winola, Belle was very dear. Her life was taken; many hearts were broken. I cannot go back and undo that horrible night. *Would telling my story add hurt? Might it bring healing?...*

Of course, another concern is that I'm not a writer. I love to share my story, one-on-one or with a crowd. But the thought of putting it all down, words on pages, was quite intimidating. I didn't know where to begin.

A friend of mine, Joe, leads a C12 group, a network of Christian CEOs in Fort Worth. He put me in touch with the senior editor of a nationally known health magazine who he said had been looking to write a faith-based story. We connected, and while this gentleman showed a genuine interest in my story, over the course of a year or so he and I never really developed any chemistry. It became clear to me as we worked that he had his own vision for the telling of *my* story.

It was Paul Vinyard who, sensing this collaborative writing relationship wasn't a fit for me, found Darin. Paul knows people just about everywhere, and he'd heard about this ghost/collaborative writer living "somewhere up North." It's a funny story to hear Darin's version of Paul's initial call: He was on vacation with his family, sitting in a beach chair with his feet in the ocean, when his cell phone rang. Darin imitates Paul's distinct baritone voice and southern charm, "Hey, bud! My name is Paul. I'm calling you from Dallas, Texas."

Darin's wife, Shari, overhearing only her husband's side of the conversation, heard, "... You say he was in prison for 35 years? For murder? Absolutely! I'd love to meet him!"

I spent nearly every morning for the next seven months developing stories from notes I'd gathered—some I'd written while I was incarcerated at SCI Rockview. Those raw notes were the beginnings of my book. Darin was able to help me put all the pieces together ... and *Unshackled* was born.

During the writing process, Darin made a few trips to work with me in Texas. We'd eat at Babe's and chip away at the story. We met a few times in Pennsylvania, revisited and retraced my steps, and we sat out in my sister Mary's yard, whittling away. We connected with old friends like the Deputy Director of Probation for Wyoming County, Jim Neary, who was instrumental in my release. Jim helped us view the story from the court's perspective. We even returned to the Marine Room, the scene of the crime; it felt like hallowed ground to be there again after all those years.

I would liken the writing process to labor—a months-long gestation period where the story is developing, and then full-out contractions come the closer you get to being done. Everyone who knew I was writing would ask, "When will the book be out?"

I came to dread the question. The emotional answer was always, "Not soon enough!"

As Paul says, though, the Lord provided everything and everyone I needed in His perfect timing. A little committee of people came together—friends like the Vinyard family, David Ford, Chris and Roni Baer, Richard Harmer—all working with me and Darin to make this book happen. Paul referred to our team as the *Book Club*.

I'd never realized all that goes into publishing—permissions, title, layout, design, subtitle, cover art, back-cover copy, front and back matter, typesetting, fonts, paper, binding, categories, genres, endorsements, a Foreword and so much more. A whole lot of ducks to get in a row—I'm very grateful for my team. I was reminded of what I'd heard the Lord tell me once in the prison chapel as we rehearsed a ministry play: "Relationships are more important than your projects."

My friend Scott Avery put the process in perspective for me one day. We were talking on the phone and he asked me, "How's the book coming along?" I happened to be at a particularly frustrating point in the process, and I complained about how long it was taking—this had gone on several months longer than I'd anticipated.

"Let me get this straight," Scott said. "You spent how long? Thirty-four years, nine months and 15 days in prison before you were released ... and now you're complaining about a couple of months?"

I excused myself from the call pretty quick: "Hey, let me get off the phone. I'll talk to you later." I spent the next several minutes praying. Scott helped me see that *I was rushing the Lord*. On one hand I was saying, "I want to do Your will." On the other, I was pressing, "Hurry up!"

The book's title was another discovery. I had a title in mind, something I'd discussed with Pastor Larry before I'd ever written a word: *AK4192: Prisoner of the Lord*. (AK4192 was my prisoner identification number, given to me the day I arrived and with me until I walked out the door a free man.) I really liked that as a title and held on to the idea through many of our early Book Club meetings.

Then, during one of our planning sessions, Paul spoke up saying, "I think we need to discuss a new title." I was open to the counsel of the team the Lord had assembled, but at heart, I really didn't want to let go of *my* title. Discussion around the table seemed to concur. Although we didn't come up with a final title that night, I knew Paul's comment and the thoughts of everyone else on the team were valid. Later that evening as I prayed, I felt the Lord encourage me, "Don't grip your title too tightly."

In June of 2016, Pastor Greg and Cathe Laurie of Harvest Christian Fellowship in California visited Babe's in Arlington. They came in to shoot a commercial to promote an upcoming Harvest Crusade at AT&T Stadium. Darin was in town, too, as we were just finalizing the manuscript. When the commercial shoot was finished, Greg and his crew sat down to enjoy some Babe's chicken. Paul asked me to share a little of my story with them. There were probably 20 or so of us gathered around the tables. When I was finished speaking, Pastor Greg said, "You should write a book!" We all laughed! Darin explained that we were nearing completion of the manuscript. "What's it called?" Greg asked. We told him we hadn't decided on a title yet.

"You should call it *Unshackled*," Cathe said, referring to the anonymous shout that was heard in the courtroom immediately after the judge's ruling.

Darin spoke up next, asking Pastor Greg, "Would you be willing to write a Foreword for Gene's book?" And he agreed.

Just like Paul said: The Lord provided *everything* and *everyone* I needed *in His perfect timing*—including the book's title and the man of God who would pen a Foreword for me. He is, after all, *Yahweh Yireh*: The Lord God, our Provider.

Then ...

The day finally arrived. I watched the truck back up to the dock and offload 6,500 copies of my book into the warehouse. It was an exciting time! I couldn't wait to see it—I was pulling back the plastic wrap as the first skid hit the floor. My first thought was, *Is this for real? My book?* And then, I was overwhelmed with real gratitude. The book looked great! It felt great in my hand! Heavy, too!

The truck driver asked whose book it was, and the general manager pointed to me. "What's it about?" he asked. After hearing I had been in prison for 34 years, he asked if he could buy one. I signed a copy for him—the first of many copies I'd sign for people. I'm glad, looking back, that this man, driving his truck from Tulsa, OK, to Gainesville, TX, received the very first, ever, signed copy of *Unshackled: From Ruin to Redemption.*

Writing *Unshackled* was really an amazing experience. It gave me a bird's-eye view of how God, over many, many years, had been present and faithful in my life. I caught a glimpse of His purpose and a renewed confidence that "he who began a good work in [me] will bring it to completion at the day of Jesus Christ" (Philippians 1:6).

The book had been out for a couple of weeks. Paul made sure copies were available at each of the Babe's locations. Occasionally, guests recognized me—

"You're Bubba, aren't you?" a lady asked me as she approached, looking for a to-go box. I've been mistaken for the owner of Babe's before. It always makes me smile.

"No," I told her, "I'm Gene, the restaurant's chaplain. It's a pleasure to meet you."

"Oh," her expression changed, "you're the guy who spent 30 years in prison! *I read your book!*"

People are always surprised to learn a family restaurant employs a chaplain. I suppose it's not something you see every day. We think of pastors in churches or chaplains in hospitals or in the military—and rather cooks, dishwashers and servers in restaurants. Every introduction provides a unique opportunity.

"So, you're a chaplain," she said. "Can you pray with customers?" I told her it was my pleasure. She motioned for me to follow her back to her table—a collection of tables, actually, pushed together to seat her large family, maybe 20 members in all. She called for everyone's attention, introduced me as "the chaplain" and pointed to a uniformed police officer seated at the head of the table. "This is my son, Thaddeus. He just graduated from the Dallas Police

Academy. Would you pray over him?"

Her son's expression told me that although he was wearing a crisp uniform of authority, in this setting—in his mom's presence—he was under *her* authority. I shook his hand and said it would be an honor for me to pray for him. So I did, speaking blessings of divine favor and protection over his life and service.

After I prayed, I excused myself so they could return to their family celebration. Then it occurred to me: God just used my book to bring a perfect stranger who had spent 34 years in prison to pray over a newly hired police officer at the request of his mother, whom I'd just met a moment earlier. I give thanks for each and every one of these divine opportunities.

Back in 1991, sitting in my cell at SCI Rockview, I daydreamed up a bucket list of sorts, *100 Things I Want to Do*. One of them, I remember, was to visit the White House. While I haven't checked 1600 Pennsylvania Avenue off the list just yet, many of the real-life opportunities I have had were better than anything I'd actually put on my list.

Receiving an invite to speak to students at Penn State University was one such opportunity. I'd been out of prison maybe six months at the time. Dr. Greg Gaertner had served as Deputy Warden at SCI Rockview during my time there. He'd retired from the prison system a few years before I was released and was teaching at Penn State when our paths crossed again. He asked me to come speak to his class. As it turned out, he got sick with shingles right before my visit, so I didn't actually get to spend any time with him. I was disappointed, as it would have been so amazing to see Greg outside prison walls—to relate as men, not as inmate and Deputy Warden.

The ride to Penn State took me right past SCI Rockview. In the distance I spotted that big, white, five-story building that was my home from 1991-2012.

The section in the middle, towering up, is the Admin portion of the building; the wings off to each side house around 500 inmates. I thought of my time there—even of some of the guys I knew who were still incarcerated there. I wished I could stop in and say hi.

It was surreal walking onto Penn State's campus. I knew that God had set this up; that He had a reason for my being here this day. I was scheduled to speak and then field some questions. I tried to anticipate what people might ask—counting on the "Are you married?" question. This wasn't my first time speaking to PSU students. I'd been a part of the Inside/Out program at Rockview, where Justice-major students came over to visit us in the prison. They came to us. This time, I was coming to them. The realization of freedom, to be able to come and go now as I pleased, was really something. Confined to ... *unshackled.*

The class was super excited to see me. I felt very much at home from the moment I walked in. I shared for around 30-40 minutes and then opened the floor for questions. The students asked me a lot of thoughtful questions about prison life, how I kept my sanity over the years and how relationships work when you are incarcerated. And while it wasn't the first question, someone did ask if I was married or dating.

Another occasion came completely out of the blue. When I saw Tiffany Vinyard's name come up on my phone after 6 p.m., my first thought was, *Is everything okay?*

"Hey Gene," she began. "Dad, Joel and I are having dinner with Glenn Beck and his wife, Tania. They would like to meet you?"

"Um, sure thing. What day?" I knew the name—the television and radio personality. I started thinking through my calendar ... *Where to put Glenn Beck?*

"No. He's hoping to meet you *right now*," she said. "Could you come join us for dinner? Do you know how to get to Glenn Beck's studio? I'll text you the address and his security team will meet you at the gate."

I told Tiffany I could be there in 20 minutes, got dressed and flew out the door. On the ride over to Los Colinas, I was thinking, *Glenn Beck the conservative talk show host wants to meet me ...* and *His security team will meet me at the gate?*

Walking into Mercury Studios was a pretty cool experience in itself. Glenn likes to buy memorabilia and preserve history, so his studio is like a museum with so much cool stuff to see. Glenn, himself, has a very welcoming presence—he greeted me with a hug and thanked me for joining them for dinner. Apparently, Paul had mentioned recently hiring me as a chaplain, as well as the little detail of my having been imprisoned 34 years, nine months and 15 days for a murder I didn't commit. That's when Glenn said, "I'd like to meet this chaplain!" So here I was, having supper with Glenn Beck. As my friend Surf says, "Gene, you just can't make this stuff up!"

I shared my testimony over dinner. In a lighter-hearted moment, Glenn asked if I was married—and we all laughed. I told him this is one of the desires of my heart the Lord hadn't seen fit to fulfill, at least *yet*. He suggested he could help find me a wife. I teased, "Couldn't hurt!"

After supper, Glenn invited us all back into his office. Like his studio, his office is filled with collectables and historical pieces worthy of a gallery. He has a huge portrait of Abraham Lincoln made out of 180,000 nails. I couldn't stop staring—what a magnificent work of art! And there, on his coffee table, I saw a copy of *Unshackled*. We scheduled a time for me to record an upcoming podcast, affording me the opportunity to share my testimony with Glenn's audience. In all, this experience was another of those *If the guys could only see me now* moments.

I'd have several of those moments related to the book. I got a call from *The 700 Club* television program. I'd seen it on TV all those years, and I remembered many of the guests and their stories—it was a humbling honor to be invited on as a guest. They bought me a ticket, rented me a room and really rolled out a red carpet for me. I got off the flight and saw a man holding a card reading *Mr. Gene McGuire*.

Everyone there was so attentive to my every need. Right off the bat, I discovered I'd lost my ID somehow in transit. The lady who had organized my trip said not to worry—they'd use my book with a photo of me on it to get me checked into the hotel. Meanwhile, my friend Chris ran over to my apartment, grabbed my passport and overnighted it to me so I could fly back home.

My hosts explained to me that they'd planned two interviews: one casual sit-down conversation and one news-type interview across a desk. They were also going to do some ad-lib taping in front of a green screen for promotion. It was a pretty busy day and an astounding experience for me top to bottom—green rooms, make-up chairs, lights and cameras. The folks serving behind the scenes were so wonderful. They get to meet everybody who comes in, and you can tell they all bring servant's hearts to their jobs. It was my privilege to make their acquaintance and share my story as a guest on their program.

Dr. Adam C. Wright, the president of Dallas Baptist University, invited me to come and share my testimony with the DBU student body. It was a beautiful chapel-service setting. Having to adapt and adjust what I can share in different settings and within different time allotments is always an adventure. I only had about 20 minutes to address this crowd, but they'd planned some discussion time afterward. This opportunity brought me face-to-face with several students whose fathers were incarcerated. They were so receptive, asking me questions like *How can I reach out to my dad?* I was so encouraged—these incredible young adults were pioneering a very different path for their lives; a path to fruitfulness and making a positive impact for God's Kingdom. I walked away from my DBU encounter feeling like the students there blessed me more than I'd blessed them.

I've had the privilege of meeting some really incredible people and ministering alongside some amazing men and women of God. If you asked me who I've met and personally known to have the greatest impact in changing the destiny of lives, it would be Amy Ford. Amy is co-founder and president of *Embrace Grace* and the author of a little life-changing, life-saving book, *A Bump in Life*. Her message is that while pro-life is a stance, being pro-love is an action. Amy's work inspires both churches and individuals to love single moms unconditionally.

I met Amy and her husband, Ryan, through my boss, Paul Vinyard. Paul had a dream one night where he was sure the Lord told him, "I want you to do something about all these young women aborting babies." Paul was like, "Lord ... I make chicken!" Paul shared his vision with a friend, David, who said, "You need to meet my daughter-in-law, Amy."

Amy's story is so familiar: conservative family, religious upbringing ... pregnant as a teenager and scared to death, she made an appointment to have an abortion. As she was being checked in and prepped for the procedure, she had a panic attack. The nurse said, "Honey, your blood pressure is up. Today is not your day. We'll have to reschedule you." Order a copy of Amy's book. And love someone in need.

I'd attended a few Teleios Men's Summits over the years. It was a huge honor when Larry asked me to open the Summit at California State University in Northridge, CA. I was very excited for the event. We prayed for weeks that God would show up, change futures and give men the courage to stand fast in their faith. The conference's theme that year was *Step Up*. I could relate—

A month or so after I received Jesus Christ as my Lord and Savior, I vividly remember kneeling on the floor of my cell and making a commitment to be an example before other men in the prison—that they would see Christ in me. The motivation for this commitment was provided by an NBA All-Star known as the *Round Mound of Rebound*. Charles Barkley was an imposing player in his day. On the court, he had sort of a bad-boy reputation.

On this particular occasion, Barkley had dominated both the offensive and defensive boards. In a postgame interview, a reporter commended him for his athletic abilities on the court and followed up by asking if he felt any obligation to present a better on-court example for younger players who looked up to him. His response was halting to me; he said it wasn't his responsibility to be an example for anybody, only to play basketball to the best of his ability and help his team win. Period.

Isaiah 43:7 spoke to me as I pondered his reply: "... everyone who is called by my name, whom I created for my glory, whom I formed and made." This was God's will for me. I was created *for His glory*. I am to give others around me an accurate account of who Jesus is, leaving a favorable impression of my God through my faith—an authentic picture of a life surrendered Jesus. In other words, I was called—*we are all called*—to Step Up.

The opening night of the Summit, before the doors opened, we spent an hour in intense prayer walking the auditorium, quite literally praying over every seat and that God would reveal Himself powerfully to every man who would sit in those seats. HOPE's House and my friend, Pastor Charles Humphrey, opened the conference, bringing the crowd to their feet in praise and worship. Then a team from Encounter Church in Las Vegas led us in song. The atmosphere was so positively charged, it felt to me like heaven had descended into the auditorium. You could feel the power and presence of God. It's at that point I was introduced.

The entire time I shared, you could have heard a pin drop. The men listened intently, leaning forward, on the edge of their seats. As I spoke, I became even more aware—and even more in awe—of the miracle God worked in my life, releasing me from a life-without-the-possibility-of-parole sentence. It was like I was reexperiencing my own wonder at God and had the great privilege of sharing it with all these other brothers.

One thing I have noticed in sharing my testimony is that I can never predict how people will respond. I have heard of instances where immediately, as I'm speaking, God sets someone free from anger or someone accepts Christ as Savior. I've also had people contact me by email later—with days, even weeks, gone by yet God continued to work in their hearts. I have this undying confidence that, when we pray and obey, the results are His responsibility. And the results always surface in His perfect timing.

During a time of altar ministry after I shared, I noticed a guy standing in about the third row back with a look of amazement on his face. I walked over to him, offered my hand and introduced myself. He explained he was an Uber driver, and he was taking the rest of the night off after two guys he'd picked up at LAX encouraged him to come. We didn't talk long. He thanked me, saying that my message had helped him.

I might not have even remembered the encounter, except the following day at a team luncheon two friends of mine from Dallas, Woody and Aaron, told the story of how they'd arrived at the airport late, and the ministry van had already departed. They chose to take an Uber for the long ride from LAX to Northridge University. Their driver asked what brought them to California. As they explained, they invited him to join them at the Summit. Saying that he appreciated the invite, he told them he had a family to feed and really needed to work the rest of that Friday night. Woody and Aaron looked at one another and immediately dug deep, pulling out whatever cash they had on them. They dropped $400 on the seat so that driver could take the rest of the night off. I sat there smiling—*I'd met their driver.*

Once the Summit concluded on Saturday night, Charles Walker, an anointed saxophonist, and I drove a couple hours to New Life Community Church in Oxnard. Pastor Steve Abraham invited us to minister at each of their four morning services.

I got up early to pray over the services. I had a very distinct feeling I was in for another powerful experience, but not created by my prayers. After breakfast we headed to the church, and I saw the basis for what I'd felt earlier—this place was a house of prayer!

After they welcomed us with hugs and cups of coffee, we circled up in the lobby where about 30 volunteers gathered to worship and pray over the service. This was fiery and powerful, and the presence of God was incredibly tangible. Unmistakable.

After praying, Pastor Steve introduced me to everyone as a guest speaker from Texas, saying, "Gene will be sharing his awesome testimony this morning."

With a big smile, I responded, "After that powerful time of prayer, I think all I can possibly add this morning is, *Amen! Let's go to lunch early.*" It was that real. As we'd prayed, I felt a heart-agreement with these dear brothers and sisters. It was almost like an unspoken thing, though we were speaking— praying. There was a feeling of unity in our prayer that was electric—like winds of the Holy Spirit blowing through the temple. You know that story in Acts 4 where, as the believers prayed in one accord, the house where they were meeting began to shake? It felt like that in my spirit before the Lord.

This prayer time always serves as a pre-game pump-up. Yes, I always have some jitters before I speak, as the adrenaline begins to flow. I realize each time what a privilege it is. I was excited for that service, anticipating what was about to happen. *Someone here is going to be blessed! Someone here is going to overcome a struggle or a hardship! God is going to show up and do God things in people's lives and hearts!*

If the pre-game was thrilling, kick-off was over the moon. A thousand people filed in, uniting their hearts in worship and their voices in praise. This place was hopping: hands raised, embraces, tears. *Wow!* At one point we sang the lyrics "I can feel the ground shake beneath us, as the prison walls cave in." I was standing next to the pastor—I was literally jumping up and down! Again, that thought dawned: *How am I going to follow THIS?*

Between services, Pastor took me back to his office to rest and pray. We had about 20 minutes. One of his staff members brought back a few copies of my book they were selling in the lobby. Some people were asking if I'd sign them. I was honored and offered to go out to the table and sign them all. Pastor said, "Gene, if I let you go out there, we won't get you back for the next service." This was hard for me to hear. I've always had this conviction to be available. But he is the pastor and knew this setting best. The more I've gotten to know Steve and his wife, the more I understand why he has such a vibrant congregation.

After the second service, he had some of the security team escort me out to the lobby where people were lined up to buy copies of *Unshackled*. I couldn't have been happier to shake hands, chat, pose for pictures and sign books for them. My attendant had an earpiece in, to give him a countdown and firm directions: they wanted me back in the pastor's office six minutes before the next service. I was relieved to get through the line in the time allotted and not leave anyone out.

The last service was incredible. Many people crowded the altar, hungry for the Lord. Because it was the last service, I was able to take more time meeting people and signing books. The warmth and hospitality I experienced was truly unforgettable.

We extended our stay a couple of days at Steve's request. He and his son, Ryan, showed us around the Oxnard and Santa Barbara areas. They took us to the Serra Cross in Ventura, overlooking a beautiful coastal view. A constant flow of people visit there and take pictures. I was no exception. We also had a divine appointment—

As we approached the tall wooden cross at the end of a well-manicured lawn and concrete pathway, a young couple recognized the New Life t-shirt Steve was wearing. The young lady made some sarcastic comment about church and rolled her eyes. Steve asked if she was familiar with the New Life community. An open bottle of beer in her hand, and with slurred speech and phrases punctuated with profanity, she told him: "I don't get along with church" and "My mother sings in a church choir."

Steve didn't try to justify the church, but rather offered an apology that she'd been hurt. Tears filled the girl's eyes. Her mascara began to run. She took another sip of her beer and asked if she could speak to Steve privately for a moment—the two of them stepped several feet away from me and the young man who was with her, a very pleasant fellow who appeared to care deeply for the young lady. After several moments, I looked up from our conversation to see Steve praying for the young woman, and then they returned. Her countenance had changed. Now she smiled behind her tears. She set down her beer and gave us a hug, thanking Steve for his willingness to listen to her and pray.

Later, Steve shared with me that when she was a teenager, a youth leader sexually assaulted her. When she finally found the courage to tell her mother what had happened, her mother's response was not to report it, saying, "You will get the pastor's son in trouble."

My heart ached at the thought of this young lady being violated ... then being *ignored* by the people she trusted to help her. I was grateful for this divine encounter—and hopeful God was at work in bringing healing. It seemed to me like one of those moments when you see the needle move in someone's life. I'm not sure what ever became of that conversation and prayer, but you can never go wrong loving people, being kind and caring. It is never a wasted investment.

My heart sank directly into my gut. A woman who had purchased *Unshackled* through Amazon left a scathing review. Reading her words, my stomach knotted tighter with each sentence:

> *Mr. McGuire participated in the killing of my aunt's sister, who owned the bar. After reading his book, I wrote Mr. McGuire an email (several email addresses were given in the book). I was forgiving but wanted to talk to him. What a crock! Never received an answer! Seems Mr. McGuire is only interested in corresponding with those who praise him. How interesting Mr. McGuire found himself in the unique position of accepting Jesus after committing the crime. He and his cousin should both be in jail for the rest of their lives. This man and his cousin caused my aunt much, much pain and depression. Karma, baby! Nobody rides for free.*

She was a relative of the victim. She had every right to address me. The only other relatives of Belle's that I'd known approached me on the day of my release—two of her nephews, whom I had the privilege of meeting. My first thought was that I'd never seen an email from her. I had no recollection of anything like this. I quickly searched old emails but came up blank. I contacted members of my ministry team and shared her painful yet heartfelt review and returned to searching.

I did eventually locate her original email, and in fact *I had read it* a year earlier. Her email was very direct, but very gracious. I shared her original message with my team, recalling that I'd planned to reply to her but dropped the ball. I had no excuse and no explanation. Now, two apologies were in order.

All the years serving my sentence, I'd never known Belle had any family members to whom I could be accountable. Besides the Lord and the Commonwealth of Pennsylvania, I didn't know who to apologize to. My court transcripts were all styled *The Commonwealth v. Eugene McGuire*.

Over the years, I'd known several fellow inmates whose victim's family members protested strongly against their release. I'd known a few whose victim's families actually sought reconciliation.

Warner—Big Moses—was the first I'd heard of like this. A victim's family member sat down with Warner and, after some heartfelt communications, came to express love and concern for him.

I had experienced a taste of this. Just moments after my release, the now former Asst. District Attorney, Jerry Idec, approached me. "Gene," he said, "these two gentlemen would like to meet you." He spun me around and I was face-to-face with two men, perhaps in their 60s.

They extended their hands, one at a time. "I know you don't know us," one of them said, "but we are both nephews of Isabelle Nagy. Our mother has written to the governor many times in support of your release over the years. We just wanted to share that with you and wish you well, now that you've been released."

I was so humbled by their comments. They weren't angry or even opposed to my release. It was as if, in that setting, God was continuing to show me His goodness; everyone and everything seemed to validate my release from a life sentence.

Everyone has fears. I had feared coming face-to-face with family members or friends of my victim. What if they wanted me to die or rot away in prison? I'd also reconciled in my heart that, should an encounter ever happen, they had every right to feel that way, no matter how remorseful I felt. Family and friends hurt by the murder of an innocent woman have every right to express their pain. My remorse should never interfere with how they feel.

After reading this dear lady's Amazon review, I realize hurt and anger over my crime do exist, and there is nothing I can do. I am truly sorry for the death of Isabelle Nagy at the hands of my cousin and how she suffered. Harm was never my intention.

During my early years of incarceration, a fellow lifer wrote a play and was looking for volunteers to take on roles. He asked me to help. I was pretty shy, definitely not wanting to be an actor on a stage, and everything in me was saying, *No way!* Yet when my friend asked, my response was, "Sure, I'll help."

The play was called *Circles of Nod*, and its message was anti-capital punishment. SCI Rockview was where lethal injections were given to men like Keith Zettlemoyer, Leon Moser and Gary Heidnik, all while I was housed there in the late '90s.

Of all the roles to play, I was given the part of a grocery store clerk who would be murdered by a drug addict during a robbery attempt. Everything in me bristled at this. How ironic to be standing in this position, behind a counter, being robbed. I could not help but imagine the fear and the pain Belle must have experienced during those moments.

Trying to get into character, someone suggested, "Think how your victim felt when you murdered her." In my heart I said, *I didn't murder anyone*. I thought that would make it easier. It didn't. This was horror—I actually tried to put myself in Belle's shoes and *feel* the dread. Try as I might, I couldn't embody

91

her experience, because at the end of *my* scene I jump up and make my way off stage ... and hear the director say, "Great job!"

There have been times when friends of mine have tried to lessen my involvement in the crime at the Marine Room in June of 1977, even to the point of saying I am *innocent*. I've never, nor will I ever, feel that way. Occasionally I've butted heads with PR folks writing bios and blurbs about me, saying I'd *suffered* for spending years in prison unjustly. *Suffering* isn't what happened to me. A moral transformation took place in my heart ... a process that taught me the importance of sound character, integrity and walking in love unfolded over those years. Without those years, I may never have encountered Jesus Christ, who redeemed my life from a pit and gave me purpose. I have asked people to change their wording, to remove the word "innocent."

Some have disagreed, arguing, "You never killed anyone." This is true; I did not take a life with my hands. I never intended for Belle to be hurt, nor did I believe my cousin would have killed her that night. But I was aware of what he intended to do—to rob her. While not willing to do it myself, I went along and participated as an accessory.

On another occasion, a woman posted comments on a Facebook page where my book appeared. She commented that her mother and Belle were good friends, and that Belle's death caused her mother much sorrow. She went on to say that I was a murderer, and worse—she was grossly misinformed about elements of the crime. A few hometown folks much more familiar with the details tried to correct her. My heart just hurt, and I wasn't sure how to help. Darin actually reached out to her, as one who had collaboratively written *Unshackled* with me, and was able to share some details from the case file to correct the misinformation she'd heard. A few days later, she voluntarily removed her comments and reached out to me with an apology. She shared with me that she was especially sorry because she knew the Lord's forgiveness firsthand in her own life. She, too, was dealing with a lot of pain.

I am grateful to have had the opportunity to connect with a few of the ones hurt as a result of my crime. Their hurt is valid. Their feelings matter. Their words are received and deeply felt.

Escorted by local Sheriffs into arraignment hearing in July 1977.

Just because everyone loved my Mom and Sister Mary and this picture.

2007- Ministry leaders with Chaplain Reitz at SCI Rockview, from left: Big Moses, Suave, me, Chaplain, Orlando, and Will (Surf).

April 2012-Moments after my release.
Freedom!

With Rob moments before entering SCI Phoenix
to share the gospel and see "Surf"

Hanging out with Henry in front of Pat's in
South Philly.

Brother Will Hull aka "Surf" receiving his
degree in Theology.

At "JIK's" in N. Phily! Orlando, Henry,
Me and JIK.

With Hamer and Henry who drove three
hours to Mansfield University to catch
my speaking event.

Hugging and not letting Steph go. .

A quick selfie while Henry who led Orlando and I through Society Hill.

Flying American with Rob first class to Dallas. April 29th 2012.

Embrace Grace fund raiser with James, Trina and Larry.

Everyone arriving at Rob's home in Dillsburg, PA, Rob, Me, Orlando, Raffy, Louey and Darin.

At the Oval with Henry, Hammer and Orlando.

Patty, Rob and I planning our trip into see the men at SCI Phoenix.

Spending Christmas with Mark and Stephanie back home.

My weekend at New Life Community Oxnard, CA. Andrew, Charles, Ryan, Pastor Steve and myself.

Some of the students attending the NE Pennsylvania Youth For Christ Fund Raiser.

Sharing a quick story with one of the Babe's Sever in Cedar Hill.

Paul made certain that each employee received a copy of Unshackled. With the servers at Babe's in Granbury, TX

A few stellar servers at the Babe's location in Arlington, TX

I love meeting the youth of my home town of Tunkhannock, PA

Meeting Laura Buffington Keiser and her family at TAHS.

Always enjoy fellowship and conversations with Gabe at Babe's Frisco.

Spending time with Brant and Jason and some awesome servers at Babe's in Granbury.

Sharing at Grace and Glory Outreach Hunlock Creek, PA

Praying for students at Christ For The Nations in Dallas, TX

Montrose High School Assembly. Montrose, PA

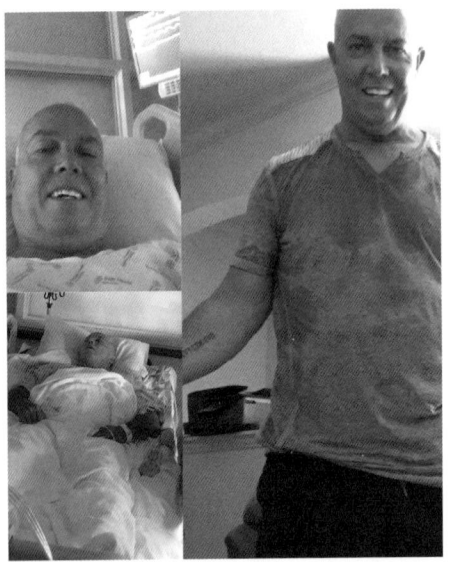

This photo captures the three days during and after my stroke.

Speaking to a group of Christian business owners and leaders in Frisco, TX

Spending few minutes during Tiger Football game with the sophomores.s

Ministering during one of four services at New Life Oxnard, CA

Sharing and being embraced by many from my home town of Tunkhannock, PA

Speaking at the NEPA Youth For Christ Annual Fund Raiser.

The evening my sister Mary passed away, I spoke with my home community at Mill City AG.

Meeting family (Cousins) during my sister Mary's memorial. .JPG

Kelsey and Jake's wedding in Wacco, TX

Planing session for LIFE after...weekend at Rob's home when I baptized Darin's Laptop with my coffee.

Embracing Pastor Jeffress after sharing my testimony at Dallas First Baptist.

Anointing service during the Men's Teleios services in North Ridge, CA

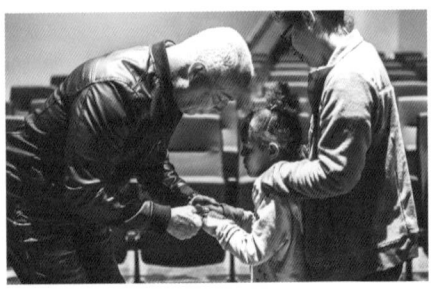

This wonderful Mother asked me to pray for her child.

With my closest friends at the Courage In Chaos Men's Conference at Dallas First Baptist. l-r Richard, James, Me, Jay and Don

With Larry praying for students at CFNI in Dallas, TX

Sharing my testimony with the students at CFNI in Dallas, TX

CHAPTER 6

THE QUESTION

Are you married?

I should pause here to reflect and ruminate on this most often asked question ... its typical follow-up, *Do you have a girlfriend? ...* and frequently accompanying offers to play matchmaker: *I may know somebody ...*

The truth is, I enjoyed the love-life inquiries and banter initially. After a while, though, I grew pretty tired of hearing it. *Why is this so important to people?* It *is* important to me. I've prayed faithfully that, in the right timing, God will bring just the right woman into my life. And I'll be honest with you—I've been looking. Show me a sign, Lord! *Any sign!*

But let me give you a little backstory and a bit of context.

In prison, validation doesn't come lovingly. Your manhood is measured by how well you can fight. It's measured by the length of your criminal record. It's measured by the seriousness of your charges and your sentence. And it's measured by how many women you've slept with.

In *Unshackled*, I told the story of my first conflict: Maybe a month in, 18 years old, and a guy in the cafeteria named Nookie *took a liking to me*. I landed the first blow, standing my ground. His friends pulled us apart, telling me, "You're gonna fight Nookie tonight on the block." Later that evening, Nookie landed his response—a blindsided padlock-in-a-sock to the side of my head.

I hit the floor. Stinging pain, ringing in my ears ... and an intense focus on keeping my cool before the COs: "Who hit you, McGuire?" *No one hit me. It was just horse-play.* Keeping my mouth shut earned the respect of the guys.

I fought when I needed to defend myself, but never by choice. Certainly not for validation.

I didn't have a criminal history to speak of. When I was 14, my brother, Mike, and I took the neighbor's Austin Healy for a joyride. Law enforcement wasn't involved, but the stunt cost us a summer's worth of work on the neighbor's farm. Not exactly a reputation-building résumé in prison.

The term "lifer" speaks for itself—you've received a life sentence without the possibility of parole. In other words, you're not getting out of here. In prison-speak, "You were given a wheel." Your life inside is going to *go round-and-round.* You don't get a wheel unless you've been convicted of a homicide. In a demented way, homicide carries a higher level of respect among the other inmates.

But I had no history with women to brag about. I was incarcerated at 17. Before that? My friend Bill and I occasionally met up with some girls at the mall. There was this religious girl, Kim, who I thought was really pretty. I encouraged and persuaded her to lie to her parents and go to a movie with me … once. We got busted. She got grounded. And there it is: the history of my love life in a nutshell.

During my early years in prison, I felt a desperate need for the validation of a girlfriend.

Going in, I received a few letters from girls I'd known in school. There was a lot of "I really liked you" sort of stuff. It made me feel good; *girls liked me.* It boosted my self-esteem. I enjoyed their letters immensely, and I made sure to write them all back. You'd love it if letters from a girl translated into visits. Being that SCI Camp Hill was several hours from my home, there wasn't much chance for my high school friends—*or these girls*—to come visit.

One day, someone handed me a list with names and addresses of girls in the local area. I sat down and penned several letters. Some girls responded. Some didn't. I remember one response—the girl wrote, "If it's money you want, I don't have any!"

I met a few girls, too, through fellow inmates. You'd see a guy out on a visit with a pretty girl and ask, "Who's that?" A sister, cousin, friend—didn't matter. "Tell her I said hi the next time you talk to her."

When it worked, we'd become pen pals, writing, sharing thoughts and desires. Eventually, I started to get some visits. Every warm letter and every visit—*to have a pretty girl waiting to see you in the visitation room*—seemed to supply a little of the validation I craved.

A few of these experiences were just that ... *experiences*.

I'd written back and forth a few times with a girl named Cathy. Her letters were kind. She scheduled a visit, and I really looked forward to meeting her in person. I walked into the visiting room and saw her sitting there—a strikingly beautiful blonde, *waiting for me*. I sat down and smiled. She smiled back, but with closed lips. I noticed that as she spoke, she tried to use her lips and occasionally her hand to shield her mouth.

I finally asked, "Is everything all right?" She nervously parted her lips to reveal she was missing a front tooth.

"I got drunk at this party last night," she explained. "I sort of got in a fight with a cop."

It was pretty clear to me that the cop won. And also that Cathy and I weren't meant to be.

I was genuinely attracted to some of the girls I met over the years. Many inmates use girls like this, pressuring them to put money in their commissary accounts, or worse, to sneak in contraband. I comforted myself in that I wasn't using them like that. But I was using them—to affirm me.

It was difficult, though. Girls would talk about how they were planning to go out on a Friday night, see a movie or attend a concert with friends. Reality set in: *I'm not going anywhere. Friday night—every night—I'll be right here.* Whether it took days, weeks or months, each one of these relationships would wane. My head and heart would move on to the next pen pal.

While I desired to be honest with the girls I met, there were times when I'd end up lying to a girl, telling her I needed our visit to be short because I had a counseling meeting scheduled. In reality, I was watching the clock. My next visit—the next pretty girl—was due for a visit any moment. I was desperately trying to avoid one girl from seeing me with another.

A friend of mine was headed out for a visit with his wife. I teased, "Ask your wife if she has any single friends." The next thing I know, I began exchanging letters with Bonnie. I learned fairly quickly that Bonnie wasn't single, but rather in a failing marriage. Her husband had been unfaithful. Their marriage woes were further complicated by their having a five-year-old daughter. She told me they were hanging on for the sake of their child.

When Bonnie first started visiting me, our visits were not romantic at all. Just friendly. A few months in, however, we started developing an attraction for one another. Then, one day she shared her perspective on our relationship, saying, "I feel secure with you, like having a boyfriend I know is not out carousing." Her words really rocked my world—*She feels safe because I'm incarcerated?* Yikes! We were using each other.

Trying to develop a romantic relationship while you're incarcerated offers up many unique obstacles and challenges. Believe it or not, romance can occur. While limited in scope to letters and calls, and maybe a little hugging and kissing during visits, if you're lucky, things otherwise pretty much unfold the same way as outside prison—sharing, getting to know one another and looking forward to a time when you can finally be together.

Some jump ahead, getting married while they're still incarcerated; a prison wedding with a Justice of the Peace. It feels like, more often than not, those relationships go down in flames—when the guy gets out you hear things like, "He's a different man than he was in prison" ... or worse, "That dude emptied my bank account, stole my car and took off."

You get cynical inside; with some guys it's almost like there's a pool when you hear he's getting married—an over/under on how many weeks the bliss will last before the train wrecks.

I knew the reality of my future. There was no "soon" in it. I was in about 10 years or so when I met Sherry. She was working at SCI Camp Hill as a medical intern. I was a mail-runner, and this meant that I got to talk to people in the medical area pretty frequently. Sherry and I became friendly. On the last day of her internship, she pulled me aside and said, "I've really enjoyed getting to know you. Maybe we can write. Maybe I can come visit you."

Sherry and I grew pretty close in the months that followed. She is an amazing girl. My heart was really in this relationship. Then one day during a visit she told me, "I've spoken with my father about you." She went on to say she'd been doing some thinking, and "waiting another five or so years for you wouldn't seem too long." I loved the sentiment but hated the thought of this dear young woman I cared about putting her life on hold, indefinitely, for me. I ended our relationship. It hurt.

For several years I ran this cycle: as soon as one relationship wound down, correspondence started with someone else. This went on until I accepted Christ as my Savior. I began to pray about my desires. He made it clear to me that I was looking to a girlfriend for affirmation and validation, when in truth my value and worth were measured on a cross, where He lay down His life to redeem and restore mine. I sat down and started writing letters to the girls I'd been in touch with: "Hey! I'm a born-again believer now. I do care about you, but I don't want to be in a relationship right now." A couple of the girls wrote back and said that were happy for me.

I committed to waiting on the Lord for a relationship and not trying to start one in prison, although there was always the temptation to resort to old ways of living.

In the years since my release, I have prayed and longed to meet my bride. I hope one day to find someone whose heart, faith and hopes for the future align with mine. A *best* friend. At times I've wondered if the single life is God's will for me—you know, like the Apostle Paul, choosing to remain single and be devoted to the Lord. Yet my desire to fall in love and be married remains strong. So, I wait. Patiently. And pray. Often.

CHAPTER 7

HOMECOMINGS

I walked into Babe's North Richland Hills on a Friday night. The store was busy, and employees were running. But something felt off. I stepped into the kitchen to learn what was going on. Adriana, our kitchen manager, told me they'd just received the terrible news that one of our employees, an 18-year-old kid named James who was genuinely loved by all his co-workers, had taken his own life.

I was shocked. "Can you say something?" she asked. *Lord! What do I say?*

There are times when there aren't adequate words—this was one of them. I asked the manager to call everyone back into the kitchen, and for a brief moment the place came to a standstill. I don't recall, word-for-word, what I said. I acknowledged that we were all devastated by the loss. I promised that, as the Babe's family—and with the Vinyard family—we would pull together and find ways to help James' family, and one another, though this unimaginably difficult time. We prayed together ... and struggled together ... through the rest of the shift. I know, firsthand, the anguish of losing a loved one to suicide. I know the questions that cannot be answered. I know the soul-deep ache. I know those cruel "What if?..." questions and "If only..." contemplations. I know loss like this results in deep and enduring heartbreak, and that we would need each other to navigate the grief.

The family cries together—we also celebrate together. Not long after James' death, I was honored when one of our servers, Kelsey, asked if I would officiate her wedding. I'd known Kelsey and her fiancé, Jake, for a year or so and was thrilled they asked me to marry them.

Jake is a soft-spoken young man who worked hard during the week so he and Kelsey could enjoy their weekends on the water—you'll find him in his boat or on his wakeboard, batwing-to-blind, on Ray Roberts Lake year-round.

During pre-marital conversations, they said they wanted a simple ceremony without a lot of bells and whistles. I asked them to script their wedding vows out and promised I'd handle the rest. The day came—Jake and I stood together at the front of the Phoenix Ballroom in Waco waiting for his bride to appear. When she did, I heard Jake sniffle, fighting back tears of joy. When we got to the vows, tears were flowing. I waded in: "Do you, Jake, take Kelsey to be your lawfully wedded wife? Do you promise to love and cherish her, to provide for her and protect her above all else ... *even your boat?*" With Kelsey's quick wit, she added an emphatic "Amen!" Everyone chuckled, including Jake. And of course, he said, "I do!"

There are also exciting company events to share as the Babe's family. Each year, we reward and honor employees who have excelled in their responsibility with a special banquet. We send limousines to pick up a hundred or so employees and drive them to a beautifully prepared location for a magnificent dinner and prize giveaway. This event is planned by the Vinyards each year because they recognize that the company's success is directly tied to those dedicated employees who uphold the family-friendly culture they've developed and nurtured all these years. The managers and kitchen staff, the servers and greeters—these are the people who make Babe's. I have to say, it is a blessing and a privilege to work for an organization that focuses on what matters most—people and relationships.

I had a quick trip to Pennsylvania planned for the upcoming weekend—several speaking engagements and officiating a wedding were on the agenda. I'd spoken with Mary on the telephone a week or so earlier and she joked with me, "You're going to be too busy to see me!" She knew better. I told her to plan on doing lunch with me—I'd stop at the lakeside diner and grab us some take-out.

"Next Tuesday afternoon, then," she said. "It's a date."

Two days passed. I was sipping my morning coffee, thinking through the busy itinerary and what I'd need to pack for the trip when my telephone rang. It was my nephew Mark. "Uncle Gene..." I knew something was wrong by the tone of his voice. "They're taking Mom to the hospital. They're putting her in the ambulance right now." *What in the world?*

Mary had been dealing with a cold for several days. Not only was she not improving, but she'd taken a drastic turn for the worse. "She can't breathe, Uncle Gene." I heard the urgency in Mark's voice, and in the commotion in the background as his mom was being wheeled out of the house. I told him I'd call the airline, move my flight up and be on my way immediately.

I was in disbelief as we hung up. I'd just seen my sister in August for her birthday, and she looked pretty good. She was battling cancer, and although I knew it was a life-and-death struggle I was confident she was going to beat it. Plus, I'd just spoken to her a few days ago—she sounded fine. How could things have progressed so fast? My hands were shaking as I searched for the airline's number and my ticket information.

My sister had been diagnosed just ten months earlier. She'd been visibly limping—and if you knew Mary, she never made a big deal out of such things. She figured it was just aging or that maybe she'd developed some arthritis in her hip. It was her mother-in-law who convinced her to go see a doctor. She was fast-tracked from that point: her doctor sent her for an MRI ... and then referred her to an oncologist.

Mary's oncology appointment actually took place during another of my previous Pennsylvania trips. I was there the day she returned from her appointment. She and Joe walked in the house, and their expressions told us the news was serious. "It's Stage IV," she said. "They say there's not much they can do."

I didn't want to believe her. *No! Heck NO!* My thoughts ran a mile a minute, trying to process what she was saying. *Is Stage IV the worst? There must be a Stage V, right?*

"Well, Jesus will heal you!" I said almost instinctively. "And then we'll all have a great testimony to share!" I know Jesus heals. I knew He'd heal my sister. That's all there was to it! I took my sister's hand and prayed, "Father, by Jesus' stripes we are healed! I send forth Your word, Lord! Heal Mary! Destroy this cancer, in Jesus' name!"

My mind continued to race—half thinking, half praying, and all-out trying to convince myself my sister would be all right. The Lord has so often blown me away with His goodness and power. Of course, He would do it again this time! I couldn't even imagine that He wasn't going to surprise me—*us*—again.

I was really grateful that my friend Richard had made that initial trip with me. This visit—when Mary received her diagnosis—was occasioned by my having just completed *Unshackled: From Ruin to Redemption*. Richard and I had flown up, Darin was on his way over to meet with us—the three of us were going to put our heads together on the book's launch. God, obviously, had other timing in mind. Richard had watched his dad battle lung cancer. As such, he was conversant in all the cancer language; able to comfort Mary and help us all interpret what the doctor had said.

Richard shared his family's story. Mary never took her eyes off him, hanging on every word. Clearly, she understood how serious this was. All the while, I sat there thinking, *Okay, how do we get you healthy?*

At one point I asked, "What about treatment?"

As the words crossed my lips, I saw Mary raise a glass to hers—"Wait! Is that soda?" I barked. "You can't drink soda, Mary! That stuff is loaded with sugar! Don't you know cancer feeds on sugar?" I said it with more force than the prayer I'd offered earlier. My dear sister had just received the worst news possible, and here I was scolding her! I immediately regretted it. I felt terrible.

In the moment, I had recalled a health and wellness class I attended in prison—the presenter graphically illustrated how much sugar is in a single serving of soda and how bad it is for our health. That's all I saw: my sister adding fuel to the cancer fire. And the look on her face—so many things I could have said ... and I chose *that*?

I don't remember a lot about that visit beyond my sister's diagnosis. Richard, Darin and I met for a few days planning the release of *Unshackled*. We talked about the possibility of doing a book launch in Pennsylvania, where all the events took place. We went to the courthouse to visit with Jim Neary, hoping to learn about non-profit organizations that were working with troubled youth, thinking we might plan a release party to benefit a local charity. We retraced my steps on the day of my release, right down to walking Clay Street end-to-end. We even revisited—again—the old Marine Room Inn, this time to walk Richard through my crime scene. I was there with them physically, but my mind was on Mary. *She* was the reason God had me here at this time.

Things settled down a bit in the weeks that followed. The doctors did have a course of treatment for my sister to follow, and Mary, with Joe right by her side, resolved to fight this thing. My faith buoyed me. I'd seen God do some pretty astounding things. I expected she was going to overcome the odds—beat this cancer.

Time passed. Having just seen Mary for her birthday back in August—10 months *after* the diagnosis and seeing how good she looked—this urgent call from Mark caught me totally off guard.

As I was on the phone with American Airlines changing my flight, eternal life came to my mind. If this was the end of Mary's battle, she'd be first to see our mom in glory. I was confident my sister had confessed Jesus as Lord—she'd go to heaven when she left this life.

I got on the early morning flight, grabbed a rental car and was at the hospital by early afternoon. The entire trip, I was praying. Thinking. Remembering.

I remembered a time, not too long ago, when a young lady who works at Babe's had a heart attack. Several of us gathered at the hospital; her family was all there, along with her boss and a few of her co-workers. Her father said, "Can we pray?"

As we huddled to do so not far from her bedside, we were aware that a lot of intense medical stuff was going on around her. Right after I'd prayed and we said "Amen," all hell broke loose! Alarms went off on the instruments she was attached to ... they coded her. The commotion intensified; people ran in, doctors were barking orders, a crash cart whizzed by us. And I was like, *Was it something I said?* I felt so defeated. So desperate for this dear young lady, for her family, for everyone in the room.

Then, the commotion settled. They'd stabilized her. The doctors told us she would survive. Jury was still out on me—my own heart needed some steadying! Just then, a nurse walked over to me and said, "Thank you for praying." I thought to myself, *I don't want to pray anymore!*

So I didn't know exactly what to expect when I'd arrive in PA. I imagined it might be like that—intense prayer, life-and-death. It is hard to put into words what I was thinking and how I was feeling. I was, at the same time, fully at peace that God was in control ... and heartbroken.

Mark and his sister, Stephanie, greeted me in the waiting room. They both gave me an extra-long hug. Mark—just like his mother—wore his emotions all over his face. Things were bad. Really bad. Steph's face was focused: no retreat, like she was ready to fight through anything with her mom. She had battled through alcohol abuse a few years earlier and really grew through that experience. Here, now, I was seeing a different, stronger and much more mature Stephanie.

"Dad is with her—they have her on a respirator," Mark literally broke down as he spoke the words. All I could do was hug him. Steph wrapped her arms around the two of us. I said something like, "It's going to be all right." I knew it was ... but I didn't know how.

The three of us walked toward Mary's room. I thought to myself, *A respirator? Lord!*

Entering, I was shocked by what I saw. Mary's appearance—my beautiful sister, with her beautiful heart and beautiful soul, lay motionless, thin, pale, frail. She'd always been the first one to step up to help out and serve others, so much so that any people in Lake Winola and Mill City referred to her lovingly as "Mother Mary" for her caring ways. Now here she was, all hooked up to IVs, tubes and wires, with a respirator breathing for her.

My mind ran through different stories in Scripture. I wondered, *If I take my sister by the hand and pray like Jesus did in Mark chapter 5, "Talitha Koum!"— which means "rise up, my little sister," would Mary open her eyes, sit up and ask for something to eat?*

I prayed as Mark and Stephanie spoke loving words over their mom. Nothing miraculous happened. The machines kept on beeping.

If you've ever been in this kind of a setting, you'll know the unique sights, sounds and smells of a sterile hospital environment. It all sort of takes you back; you recall other times you've been in similar situations.

My mind flashed back to a time four years earlier. We learned that PJ, one of the general managers at Babe's, his wife and two children were in a very serious car accident. They were on their way back from Oklahoma when a driver under the influence crashed into the side of their car, killing their 15-year-old daughter, Skylar, on impact. PJ's wife, Kelly, was on life support, and their six-year-old son, Riley, was in critical condition. We rushed to the hospital to be with PJ as they fought for their lives—more than a dozen management team members and the entire Vinyard family had gathered in the waiting room. It's hard to imagine the heartache—a man keeping vigil over his critically injured wife and son, while also planning a memorial service and funeral for his daughter.

Skylar's service was beautiful. Many found comfort in recalling her faith and boldness in Christ. Her funeral was nothing short of a celebration of her short life, lived to the fullest. After the service, we turned our attention again to continual prayer for Kelly and Riley.

A few days passed. Doctors informed PJ they were seeing no signs of improvement in Kelly; hers were not injuries she could recover from. They recommended removing her from life support. PJ gathered the Vinyard family and several close friends to share the doctor's recommendation ... and his most difficult decision—to let her go. In my spirit, I felt Kelly was already gone; I knew she was with Jesus. A time was set to take her off the machines.

PJ asked Chris and me to join him at her bedside as he said good-bye. This moment is one of the hardest yet most blessed privileges I've ever experienced. We prayed. We cried. I felt the tangible comfort of our Lord and Savior in our pain. After a little while, PJ asked us to leave them alone. He said good-bye to the wife of his youth, the love of his life ... and a short while later, Kelly passed from this world, leaving her vital organs so others could live.

As I stood by my sister's hospital bed, I had this same conviction—the more I watched her, the more I prayed, it felt to me like she'd already let go. This was no longer my sister in this body worn down by cancer. Mary was ready to go home—to her heavenly home. This would be the manner in which my little sister would break free from the temporal into the eternal. I came to the realization that I was here to say good-bye.

Mark pleaded with his mom to get better. Stephanie showered her mom with assurances, "I love you, Mom!" Joe was fighting desperately to will his wife and best friend of 36 years to live on.

The doctor requested to meet with the family—and I knew how it was going to go.

"I recommend you start making arrangements," he said.

Mark and Stephanie were in disbelief: "You mean she's not going to get better? She's not going to recover? How can you be so sure?" I was heartbroken for them—this is their mother!

The oncologist explained, "When your mom first arrived at my office, she was very sick. Her body was full of cancer. Your mom never gave up, but her body has. With your approval, we will remove Mary from life support, and she will pass away on her own time—it could be immediate, or it might take a few hours. But she is *not* going to recover. This is the end." He recommended we try to get some rest and make the final decision the next day.

The doctor was right when he said Mary hadn't given up. She was hopeful. She had told me, "When I beat this, I want to visit children with cancer to encourage them." But her body couldn't handle the terrible side effects of chemotherapy and radiation treatments anymore, and they weren't making any progress against the disease.

I started thinking about my schedule and the reasons I'd made this trip—I had several speaking engagements planned for the next few days. I felt bad since churches had paid for my flights and made arrangements. I was even supposed to officiate a wedding at Grace & Glory Outreach. I had no idea, now, how any of that would be possible.

I called my friend Bill Nast and explained Mary's condition. He said everyone would understand, and that he could stand in and officiate the ceremony for me. We discussed that, possibly, I could call in to the ceremony via FaceTime. Bill loved the idea, so we penciled it in—I'd call at noon and officially pronounce them man and wife.

As we prepared to head home from the hospital, Joe suggested we grab some takeout on the way—we weren't sure we'd be hungry, but we knew nobody wanted to cook. It was a good plan. Things were quiet at the house when we got there. I walked into the living room and found Joe reclining in Mary's favorite chair, tears running down his cheeks. "Hey Joe, I'm here, brother!"

I hugged him and could feel his tears on my face. His body shook. "You'll have to do it," he said. "I can't. I'd feel like I was killing her. Will you sign the paperwork?"

All I could say was, "Whatever you need me to do, Joe. I'm here."

With heavy hearts, the four of us made the decision in the morning. It was a Saturday afternoon when they turned off the machines. It was eerily quiet in her room, just the quiet beeps of the instrument monitoring her vitals. Mary appeared to be resting comfortably, taking shallow breaths. Mark and Steph sat on the side of their mom's bed, holding her hands, saying things like "We love you" ... "We are right here with you."

At some point Mary's breathing began to labor. Her heart rate increased, and so did the beeping. It was a nerve-racking sight. Steph cried out, "Where's the nurse? She needs help!"

Joe had a horrified look on his face. He rushed out the door furiously, and yelled to a nurse, "Get a doctor in here! You said she wouldn't be in any pain! You promised me she wouldn't be afraid!"

The nurse tried to reassure us, explaining that this was not uncommon. As she quickly worked to adjust Mary's meds, Joe, Mark and Steph walked out of the room, disgusted.

In just a moment or two, as the medication did its work, Mary's breathing settled. I stood alone with my sister, and I said out loud, "I love you, Mary! You are a great mom, and a great wife to Joe." I broke down crying. Honestly, it was the first time I was overcome with emotion during the entire ordeal. The dam broke! "You did a great job," I told her. "It's okay, now, for you to go be with Jesus!" A profound peace came over me—but my heart ached for Joe and the kids.

I was able to step out of the room a little while later. We were grateful Mary had been stabilized and was no longer struggling physically, even in her unconscious state. The wedding I was to officiate was scheduled to start within the hour. The plan was for me to call in around the point where the couple was exchanging rings and end the ceremony.

I located a glass walking bridge in the middle of the hospital, directly off the ICU. I hoped it would provide me with a quiet space and strong enough

WiFi signal to allow for a good connection. When it was time, the connection couldn't have been better. I could see Jillian, the bride, and Erik there on my phone. "By the authority granted me as a minister of the Gospel," I said, "in accordance with the laws of the great State of Pennsylvania, and in the name of the Father, Son and Holy Spirit, I now pronounce you husband and wife. You may kiss your bride!"

With that, I could hear the cheers of those in the background. I also realized a small group of folks standing courteously still on both ends of the bridge—they'd undoubtedly figured out what was happening and did their best not to interrupt.

Since I knew Mary could pass at any moment, I went back to the waiting area. We waited alongside others whose loved ones were dying. A lady came over to me and said, "Thank you for sharing that beautiful moment on the walkway with us." I didn't understand what she meant. She explained that she was among those waiting to cross over the walking bridge. "It was a blessing to witness something so beautiful while we're all here, trying to come to grips with such loss."

Sunday morning, October 15th. Mary was off all life support. Joe and the kids kept vigil by her side. I was speaking at Mill City Assembly. Just as the worship service ended, Mark phoned: "Mom just passed away."

It's a strange mixture of emotions to describe. Joy, in knowing my sister was with Jesus, death has no sting; sadness, in the realization she is no longer here for me to visit, call, chat and laugh with; gratitude, for having had such an amazing sister in this life; hurt, for this fallen world we live in, where a disease like cancer takes loved ones; and hope—for while I cannot see the bigger picture, I know He has one, and He is faithful to work all things for good.

I don't guess I'd emotionally dealt with it all yet. I walked into the house, and, seeing everyone else, it was like everybody and everything was moving in slow motion. I think by emotional default, I went into *How can I help?* mode. Mark and Steph were calling people, letting them know she was gone. Family friends were coming and going, sharing their condolences. You know how that goes—lots of tears and every interaction seems to end the same way: "If there is anything I can do ..."

At some point I noticed Joe, slumped into Mary's chair in the living room, sobbing. "I want you to do the service," he said. "And I don't want no sad service. Mary's with Jesus ... and He better appreciate her." I nodded. We made some plans. I wanted to share the Gospel. I wanted to tell some stories. Thinking back through some of those stories brought smiles to our faces.

The service was packed, wall-to-wall. My cousins Barbara and Diane, and Diane's daughter Tiffany, came from New Jersey. Rob and Patty came. Hammer came. My cousin Bobby's wife, Arlene, and daughter Chrissy were there. It was a very moving time, but it was punctuated with some lighter-hearted moments as people shared their warm recollections of Mary. Afterward, we had a reception, and the stories continued, as did the gratitude in all our hearts to have been blessed with such a wonderful wife, mother, sister and friend.

Returning to my high school had been a desire of mine since the summer of 1991. I'd just gotten back from Phoenix, in the aftermath of the Camp Hill riots. I'd heard a message from legendary college football coach Lou Holtz where he encouraged the audience to make a list of 100 things we wanted to accomplish in our lifetime. I started my bucket list that evening: visit Israel; go to the beach; speak on the radio; write a book; be a guest on *The 700 Club*; get married; go to the White House; own a car; own a home; *and share my testimony at my high school.*

During a 2017 trip—the same time we learned about Mary's diagnosis— Richard, Darin and I went to Tunkhannock High School on a Friday night and took in a football game: the Tigers played against their archrivals, the Towanda Black Knights. I bumped into a few people in the stands that night who knew me; a few of the current faculty and staff members were classmates of mine back in the day. Things looked a little different—some 40 years had passed since I'd played on this field—but much of it felt haltingly familiar, as if time stood still. I wondered if and when an opportunity might arise for me to address Tiger nation. I renewed my prayers for a door to open if it was the Lord's will.

Back in April, I was invited to join a FaceTime meeting of a Tunkhannock-area book club. They'd been reading through *Unshackled*. They set up a Q&A and discussion call, and I was thrilled to participate—a virtual book club was another first for me. Near the end of the call, the host introduced me to her husband, Todd. I'd noticed him step into the room behind his wife a few minutes earlier and take a seat. He asked, "Gene, has anyone ever invited to speak to high school students?" I told him of the few opportunities I'd had to speak with students in Texas, and that I'd been praying for a chance to share my testimony at Tunkhannock High School—*my* high school—for some time.

"I can make that happen," he said. Todd revealed that he was an assistant principal there and said he'd love to have me come address the student body. I was blown away. In disbelief. I'm FaceTiming with a book club one minute, and … *Wait! Is he serious? Is this happening?*

After the call, I danced around my place, praising God, in awe of the Holy Spirit's ability to weave people and things together perfectly—right people, right places, right timing. Amazing! A few months later, after a slew of planning calls and emails back and forth, arrangements were made, and I booked my flight.

It was a beautiful Thursday evening, the night before I was scheduled to speak to the assembly of students. I was overwhelmed as I prayed about this opportunity. Few events stand nearly as tall as God's salvation in my life and the day I was released from prison … but *this*. Anticipating the next day's event at *my* high school was up there. The idea that I'm here—that the Lord set this up— that it was on *my* list; I was so grateful, humbled and amazed.

Forty years had passed since I last walked these halls. Things looked smaller than I remembered, but so much was the same. Bricks, polished floors, bulletin boards, Tiger Pride sports banners. Then a very familiar bell sounded, and students flooded the halls—it was like a flashback. Some students stopped to chat with one another, others walked with purpose. Many called out, "Hi, Mr. Bosscher!" He responded to each student by name. A few who engaged him in conversation shot me a look like, *Who is this guy wearing blue jeans, cowboy boots and a denim shirt?*

Memories flooded back as I walked those halls beside Todd. As a sophomore, I'd run these very halls during the winter months, preparing for track season. The hard floors caused nasty shin-splints ... the recollections were so strong I could almost feel the pain. Looking into classrooms I'd had as a kid ... science lab, history class, math. Surreal. Todd pointed out name plaques on some classroom doors—the names of some of my classmates 40 years ago who became teachers there.

I looked into the metal shop. More memories. Of high school, but also of those early days of my incarceration—welding was my first prison job. I had a leg up, having been in metal shop here.

We walked past my old English classroom. I really enjoyed that class, even though I got an "F" for a final grade—one of many I'd earned my sophomore year. I hated reading. I had immense difficulty comprehending what I'd read. I'd skim over sentences, paragraphs and entire chapters just to get to the end of the assignment. And I couldn't spell. I was too embarrassed to admit it.

I remembered all the struggles I'd had academically and how sports was an escape for me. On Fridays, game day, we'd proudly wear our sports jerseys to school. If you were lucky, a cute girl might wear your jersey.

The crowd in the hallway diminished. Students funneled back into classrooms. I looked for my old locker. It felt like it was just yesterday; Billy and me racing to our lockers between classes—crammed with unread books and half-completed homework ... *and Ring Dings*. Me and Billy always kept a supply on-hand to eat a fistful and head to class.

"Are you hungry, Gene?" Todd suggested we slip into the cafeteria for some lunch. More memories—the smell of cafeteria food, the sounds of utensils, trays and students. Several more students came to speak with Todd, and I was impressed how he introduced each one to me by name.

I couldn't have been prouder to have been invited back—to walk these hallways, meet today's Tunkhannock students and share my story. I was living out, in that moment, a profound answer to prayer. We headed to the auditorium as the assembly was set to start.

I knew there might be a few people I knew in the assembly, based on some of those names I'd seen. Scott Howell, for instance. He and I played football together. Now he was Mr. Howell, the history teacher. And Barb, an art teacher. My freshman football coach, Coach Davis, was still there after all these years.

The auditorium began to fill in. Freshmen came in first, followed by the sophomores. I couldn't believe we ever looked that young. As the juniors entered, it hit me: *this is the class I never saw*—I was sent to prison at the end of my sophomore year. And then the senior class filled out the remainder of the seats. My heart raced with adrenaline. I'd attended assemblies here, sure; I'd sat in those very seats as a student; and now Todd stood up to introduce *me*.

"He's one of you," Todd said, "a former Tiger, and the author of *Unshackled: From Ruin to Redemption*. Please welcome Mr. Gene McGuire."

I don't remember exactly how I started, but I never felt more at home. I didn't graduate and go on to college, but I'd made it back—I'd come home. I can still close my eyes and see their faces, their eyes, the emotional responses as I spoke that afternoon. Afterward, students gathered to thank me. One, a girl named Alex, stood out. A senior on the field hockey team, she asked several very good questions. We had a pretty good conversation, and she asked if we could take a picture.

At the close of my visit, Todd walked with me out the glass doors over to the parking lot. I looked back over my shoulder in wonder: *How many people get this chance? How many get to go back to their high school, share their testimony and see God's hand at work in, through and over some 40 years?* I drove back to my sister's house in a euphoric cloud.

On the drive, I was overwhelmed thinking, *If my friends could see me now!* It's a feeling I have often, as I've said, and each time it is very emotional. I think back to my friends at Rockview—Scott, Henry and Warner—they were so happy for me when I was getting out. Tears of joy filled their eyes. Joy for me. *"Bear! You're going home!"* I wished I could bring each of them with me.

That last night before I left SCI Rockview, a crowd of my brothers gathered around me to pray. When Scott raised his voice, he prayed, "You are going to take Gene's testimony around the country, Lord!"

I remember thinking, *Okay ... that's bold.* And now, just a few years later, the Lord had opened doors for me to speak from coast to coast. As some of my friends have been released, I've had the privilege of having Henry, Jeff and Orlando along with me when I've spoken. Several of my brothers are still incarcerated—I so wish those guys could also be with me. And not just in ministry settings. Driving down the road, taking in the sights and sounds, having a place of their own, shopping, eating out, having a job ... all the things you sit around thinking about when you're in prison, imagining.

When I made my list of 100 things, each entry was impossible at the time I wrote it. *Look at what God can do!* I often think, in those terms: *If my friends could see me now!* And I long for the day when each of them can start to realize things on their own lists and treasure freedom for the gift and luxury it really is.

CHAPTER 8

SOMETHING IS WRONG

It was sort of like waking up from one of those really good, long, deep sleeps. I was awake, but groggy. I imagined it must have been around 5 a.m. — time to start the day. I'd begin, as usual: roll out of bed and make the short walk to the bathroom. Only ... I wasn't rolling out of bed.

I struggled with the sheets and blanket that I'd wrapped over my shoulders in the night. I tried to roll, tried to free myself—only to discover *things aren't working as they should*. Reaching, pushing, pulling. *What the heck is going on?* I struggled some more, and eventually worked myself to the point of being out of breath. *Something is wrong!*

I lay there like a mummy for a moment, trying to calm down and catch my breath. *Think!* I decided to take my right hand and reach for the sheet. But nothing happened. Nothing moved. I start to freak a little bit. Confusion, fear, anger all set in. *What is happening to me? What is wrong with me?* With my left hand, I reached for my right, which I believed was lying on my chest—that's quite an alarming experience, reaching for a part of your own body only to discover it isn't where you think it is. Which meant panic set in. *Where the heck is my right hand?*

With my left hand, I tossed my covers off and discover my right arm was down my right side—it wasn't on my chest as I'd thought. Try as I might, I couldn't move it. I lifted it with my good hand, but the arm felt like it was totally asleep—pins and needles—and extremely heavy. As soon as I let it go, it flopped back down on the bed.

I put my head back, closed my eyes and tried some deep breathing, trying to sort out what was going on. Maybe my arm had just fallen asleep during the night. *Move it around—get a little blood flowing* I told myself. Then I realized, it wasn't just my arm. I couldn't move my right leg, either. I attempted to roll again, but half my body wasn't responding. I was terrified. *Am I having a stroke?*

I cried out, "Jesus! Please help me!" All sorts of thoughts ran through my mind. *This is bad. Will anyone be able to help me?*

I began to tell myself: *You need to fight through this. You've been in worse circumstances, greater pain and more alone.* Using all the strength I could muster, I reached for my cell phone on the nightstand. It was then that I noticed, it wasn't 5 a.m. ... it was 11:30 p.m.! I'd been asleep less than an hour. *What in the world is going on?*

I recalled that I'd spent the evening with friends. We'd had a great dinner and watched a movie. When I got home, I had texted them to say I made it home safely: "I'm home. Had a great time. I'm going to have the best night's sleep ever." Then I brushed my teeth and crawled into bed.

I got the phone but struggled to operate it with my left hand. Holding it to try to navigate the screen, locate and open an app to reach out for help—all while I was quite honestly panic-stricken—I tried to type the words "help me" and press send. I couldn't make anything work.

As I fought to get out of the messaging app and back to where I could make a phone call, I got a chill. I started to shiver and shake uncontrollably. I couldn't find the keypad to dial 9-1-1. Chills, out of breath, frustrated with my lack of coordination, I felt hopeless. Some 20 minutes passed before I noticed the word *Emergency* in my contact list. I touched it and heard someone say, "9-1-1, what is your emergency?"

I tried to answer, but no words came out of my mouth. I grunted, tried to clear my throat and managed only a whisper: "Help me!"

The words were too quiet to hear. She repeated, "9-1-1, what is your emergency? Can you hear me?" I began to cry and held the phone close to my mouth, hoping she'd hear me and know I needed help.

After that, it's all a blur. I know the operator kept talking to me. I can't tell you what she said, or if I was even able to say anything more to her. I heard sirens outside, and she asked, "Can you go and open the door?"

I grunted "No," unsure if she could hear me. I just cried.

Then I heard, "Fort Worth Police! Open the door!" I heard them repeat it even louder—"Fort Worth Police!"—and I cried even harder. I tried to yell with all my might, "I'm up here! Help me!" but could barely make a sound.

I was shaking uncontrollably. Freezing. Terrified. Then I heard wood splintering. They'd forced open my front door, announcing again, "Fort Worth Police!" I could hear them coming, so I tried to call to them, "In here! I'm in here!"

The police and paramedics opened my bedroom door and turned on the light. They had a million questions for me, all I could answer was, "Help me!" As they worked to stabilize me, I got to where I could nod my head to answer their questions. I felt so helpless, unable to talk, unable to get up out of bed, unable to use the bathroom.

The paramedics worked diligently, taking my vital signs, communicating with the hospital and preparing me for transport, and I began to calm down some. They got me on a stretcher, wrapped me up in blankets. I was still shaking, but I knew I was in good hands.

As they took me out the front door and to an awaiting ambulance, I noticed the flashing red and blue lights reflecting all down the block. *What must my neighbors be thinking?* On the ride to the hospital, I just tried to relax and pray.

As we arrived at the hospital, doctors and nurses tended to me with great urgency, calling things back and forth to one another, checking my left side against my right, asking me to do things like "Move this toe" and "Move that finger," all while affixing blood pressure cuffs, inserting IVs and hooking up sensors and monitors. They asked questions about my medical history, current medications, allergies and such. Everything was happening so fast, and I still couldn't manage anything more than a whisper or mumble. Eventually I was instructed to blink my eyes to answer their questions.

One of the nurses had my cell phone and asked me about the contact Larry Titus. I nodded YES emphatically. I don't know how long it took, or what time it was, but next thing I knew Larry was standing next to me. He grabbed my hand and said, "Everything is going to be all right. I prayed for you on the way over."

The nurse who had my phone said, "Amen! In Jesus' name!" She leaned over and whispered in my ear to assure me I was getting the best care possible and that the Lord had me right where I needed to be.

They sent me for an MRI and a CAT scan. A blood clot in my brain had caused my stroke. They recommended a surgical procedure and alerted me to all the risks—brain bleeding and death—and off to surgery we went.

I woke up in post-op ... and immediately tried to move my arm. It moved! It still felt heavy, but it did what my brain asked it to do! I opened and closed my hand. It worked! I started crying. I moved my foot, my leg, bent my knee. It all worked! I kept flexing muscles and moving as they rolled me from post-op to the ICU. In an elevator, the nurse asked me if I wanted to see what caused my stroke. She showed me a grainy, gray photo and pointed to a little black dot. "That's the clot we removed," she said. All the while, I was still moving under the covers. It felt good!

The doctor explained that I'd had an ischemic stroke. It was likely caused by an Afib (atrial fibrillation). I'd experienced Afib when I was in prison—it just felt like an occasional speeding heartbeat. I never thought anything of it. Going forward, the doc told me, they'd put me on blood-thinning medication, that I'd need to follow up with a cardiologist and that I should be fine. That last part was music to my ears, and a wonderful answer to my prayers. But this hadn't come out of the blue.

A month prior, I'd awakened in the wee hours of the morning with an unusually sharp, painful headache. I took some Aleve and went back to sleep. Later that morning I had a mentoring session scheduled with a youth pastor. I struggled to function through our meeting. I had difficulty reading the words in my Bible. A couple times during our conversation I couldn't express my thoughts well—my friend finished a few words and sentences for me.

By late morning, I'd made the hour-long drive north to minister at Paul's Antique Lumber Company. Feeling somewhat groggy, I shared the Gospel and prayed with some of the workers. All along, I was thinking I was just really overtired. I tried to counter my confusion by quoting memory verses, yet none came to mind. Unable to think of any, I tried remembering Bible books themselves. *Genesis, uh ... Genesis ...??* I couldn't remember what followed. *Switch to the New Testament*, I thought. I worried when I couldn't remember what followed Matthew. I told the guys I wasn't feeling well, excused myself and drove home in a fog.

Once home, I called Chris and told him what I was experiencing. He suggested I go to the ER. I declined, saying I'd lie down and see how I felt in a little while.

Orlando called to say hello. After sharing with him what was happening, he too said, "Go to the ER." He reminded me of our friend Jim, who had a stroke years earlier at Rockview. I really didn't want to hear that. Not me.

By morning, the fog seemed to be clearing some, yet I struggled through my devotion. Still reluctant to visit the ER, Tiffany Vinyard called. "Gene, please go to the ER in Fort Worth immediately. Dad and I want you to get checked by a doctor. Don't worry about the cost, we are asking you to go. Will you go?" Tears filled my eyes as I agreed, and they had Chris come pick me up.

After several tests the doctor informed me that a *mini stroke* had occurred.

It was humbling to hear the news, even though I was feeling better by the hour. Even my memory returned. They scheduled me for an MRI later that night, and I was admitted. James and Richard stayed with me throughout the day. As evening arrived, James prayed for me and headed home. I told Richard he should head home as well, but he told me he'd stick around until I had the MRI, scheduled around midnight. After the scan, I slept pretty hard. When I opened my eyes in the morning, I saw Richard had camped out on the cold hard floor, using his computer bag as a pillow. I just stared down at my friend: *How fortunate I am to have friends like this—to have him here with me.*

With results of the MRI came news that I'd had maybe a dozen mini strokes over the years. Most go completely unnoticed. They prescribed medication for me, and I returned home. A few days later I was back to full speed, back at work and feeling great. I sort of forgot about the medication. Who needs it? I've never had heart problems, I am not overweight, I've never smoked, I work out daily. I was in denial.

And now, here I was—

Larry's words when he arrived at the hospital, saying "I prayed for you," reminded me of the many times he'd visited me in prison. I'd always wander into the visitation room and spill all my issues and frustrations out. He'd listen and then say, "Pray about it." I remember in the early days of our friendship, that answer seemed shallow, like, "Sure, I'll pray about it. *But what do I do?*" In time, I learned the power of prayer. When we pray, we're placing the matter in God's most capable hands.

Through prayer, and thanks to the amazing care of the doctors and nurses at Harris Methodist, I made incredible progress over the next few hours. I was resting easy, my confusion cleared, and my speech was improving. In the morning, friends who'd gathered in the waiting area were allowed to filter into my room. I felt the presence of God in each of their visits. They were all shocked at what happened— and relieved with my prognosis and progress. My friend Chris stayed for hours. Every so often throughout the day, he'd smile and say, "Look at you!" It was great to feel the love and prayers from so many dear friends.

There were challenges, though. During one of my rehabilitation sessions—I had to retrain myself to bring a spoon to my mouth, and to walk, which was all very difficult.

The nurse commented, "We will be sending you to a rehabilitation facility for a week or two."

I said, "That's dead!"

She looked at me, perplexed, and asked, "What's dead?"

"That's dead" is an expression I'd picked up in prison. It meant, *That's not happening!*

I explained, "I'm not going to a rehab facility."

"Where do you think you're going?"

"Home," I told her. I'd seen people who've had very serious strokes and needed to be retrained in everything—how to get food into their mouths, sip from a cup and so on. I was better off than that. Anything I needed to relearn, just give me the regiment—I was confident I could do it at home.

I didn't want to embrace the limitations imposed by my stroke any more than I'd embraced the idea that I was a lifer. I believed God had a better plan.

On Sunday, my third day at the hospital, I saw both the neurosurgeon and the cardiologist. They both expressed their willingness to sign off on my release. My close friend Don Oldfield stopped in on his way home from church ... just in time. Don asked who was taking me home, and I said, "You are!" We laughed as we gathered my bags and headed out the door.

When I got home, my friend Mickey had stepped up—he'd gone to work repairing my splintered door frame and called in a locksmith to replace the lock. My friend Richard arranged his schedule so he could spend time with me during the day, even staying overnight—just to have someone around in case a need arose. Richard tasked himself with being my personal rehab buddy, peppering me all day long with memory-sharpening questions, ensuring that I was eating properly and getting me up walking—we made daily laps around my neighborhood. I regained both strength and confidence pretty quickly. It is a true blessing to have friends who genuinely care.

One of the hardest parts of this health scare for me was having to cancel speaking events I had scheduled. The churches I had planned to visit were all gracious, sharing their concern for me, and praying for me. I believe their prayers accelerated my healing and allowed me to walk in what God had already designed for me to live out.

CHAPTER 9

INSIDE OUT

I'd been out a couple of years. I was sitting in my apartment one day when I get a phone call—I don't normally answer numbers I don't recognize. This time I did. A voice says, "Geno!"

"Who's this?" I responded.

"Who do you think it is?"

I didn't know, so I guessed: "Jack Fisher?"

This guy on the phone laughs, "Well … I know Jack Fisher." I was still clueless. Finally, he says, "It's Hammer!"

Hammer was top dog in the kitchen. I was top dog down in supplies, shipping and receiving. Jack was my boss, so we all knew and saw a lot of each other. As the kitchen needed this or that, we'd order it in and get it to them.

Man! I knew Hammer had been out; he'd gotten out a few years before me. But he didn't know I was out. He told me he was on Facebook, came across a mutual friend of ours and saw a post from me—so he was like, "Gene McGuire? What? Are they letting lifers get on Facebook now?" He and his wife clicked through my profile. They saw that I'd been posting since 2012—and then they saw the posts about my release. Hammer was shocked. He found a number and called.

This was very different from my experience with Orlando. Right before I was released, Orlando was transferred to a county facility because of overcrowding. As soon as I was out, I got in touch with him. We exchanged calls and letters, and I'd put some money in his commissary account and stuff like that. Not too long after I was out, I got a chance to go see him.

There was a Deputy at the county facility who had previously been the Captain of Security at SCI Rockview. He knew Orlando and me—all us guys. Orlando says that one day that Deputy came to him and said, "Hey, I just got off the phone with Gene McGuire. He's coming to see you."

They had no-contact visiting—essentially, you'd sit with a glass partition between you. I walked in, we saw each other, and we both started crying like babies.

Orlando told me that a few months after our visit he got called to the visiting area again—this time he looked around and didn't see anyone he recognized. There was this couple sitting in one of the visitation windows looking as confused as he was. Their eyes met and they were like, "Are you Orlando?"

I'd spoken at Penn State and, in telling my story, mentioned my friend Orlando. This young couple, probably in their mid-20s, told him, "We promised Gene McGuire we'd come to visit you." I don't even remember that conversation! But they were able to visit him and blessed him with a few books. How cool is that?

Orlando got bounced around a couple more times before his release in 2018. We stayed in touch the whole time. I knew Orlando would be getting out—I think 2017 was his minimum, but there was some delay. About six months after he was released, Orlando flew down to Texas to see me. And that, in itself, was a real God thing—it just doesn't happen that a parole officer would let a parolee travel out-of-state so soon after his release.

Typically, the way parole works—Hammer and Orlando can tell you firsthand—guys with a long tail get pretty intense parole terms initially upon their release. Say your sentence is 15-30 years, you can be released for good behavior and such on the earlier side of that sentence and serve the remainder, or "tail," on parole. And there are all sorts of stipulations that only time and building trust with your parole officer can ease. For Orlando to be able to travel so soon was God's favor. He will tell you that when he asked, he wholeheartedly expected the answer to be a flat NO.

In my case, I was never on parole. Judge Shurtleff released me "Time Served." But when guys are out on parole, it can be quite a harrowing process. They often have their POs changed from time to time, and by design, so fresh eyes are looking. Just about the time you get to know your PO, and he or she gets to know you, you're given a new one.

POs only have two vantage points from which to know a parolee. The first is the criminal record, which is the basis for the relationship, or who-you-are-to-them. When a file ends up on their desk, you're a number and criminal file. That's all they've got to go on. The second vantage point is their experience of you, from Day One. It's up to you to make, and maintain, a good impression. The guys who succeed in their parole understand it is incumbent upon them to give their PO a new view, one that supplants or supersedes the criminal record.

You can imagine, however, cases in which the opposite occurs—where you have a guy with a certain history and then he starts coming up and tests with dirty urine, weed in his system or whatever, reinforcing that criminal-record impression.

When a guy gets out, the parameters are pretty stringent: maintain employment, no drugs or alcohol, curfews at 9 p.m. or whatever. The guys who take it seriously and do as they're directed succeed. The guys who buck the system from the get-go—thinking *Being in at 9 p.m. is a joke!*—they're the ones who will be back inside. And you see them come back, having violated, and it's always somebody else's fault. They'll say "it was my PO" or "my girlfriend" or "my employer" ... any excuse they can find. You'd often see guys violated for moving. They'd say, "I moved into my girlfriend's house." It's not that they can't move; it's that they didn't go through the proper process to move, alerting their PO and so on.

If you believe all the stories you hear from the guys who come back, you'd think it all but impossible to succeed out there in the real world ...

But I'm extremely proud of Henry, Orlando and Hammer. They've all embodied the challenge of re-writing the script. They're positive examples. Through the choices they make every day, they've each built structure, discipline and responsibility into their lives. Here's the fact: *It's easy to stay out! Just do what you've got to do.*

Taking on responsibility leads to maturity. Orlando and I talk about how we'd worked at prison jobs for 19 cents an hour back in the day. They become a platform—not an economic one ... *it's 19 cents an hour*! But a platform in that when you are faithful in the little things, you are given bigger opportunities. You start cleaning toilets.

Orlando talks about his resumé in prison. He started out like pretty much all inmates—scrubbing bathrooms. Over the years, he worked his way through a number of jobs, eventually becoming a dog trainer, one of the more desirable and rewarding jobs. They don't just give those jobs out to anyone. He had to show up, year-in and year-out, for all the lesser assignments, giving them his all. And he had to qualify for the dog trainer position, pass some interviews, earn approvals and learn the appropriate skills. He will tell you: had he not developed that sense of responsibility working the mundane jobs, he never would have had the bigger/better opportunity. And we both can tell you—that crappy 19-cents-an-hour job matters in the big picture. During his time in, Orlando cared for and trained 22 dogs that had been abused. You can pretty much predict that guys who have purpose in jail have purpose getting out.

There was this guy named Dennis at Rockview—he'd been in and out a number of times, and always with an explanation. He was being released on one occasion and came to a group of us in the dayroom, asking, "I'm leaving tomorrow. Brother Gene, will you pray for me?" I'd forgotten, but Orlando reminded me about what happened:

We got in a circle, and everyone lay their hands on Dennis. I prayed, "Lord, put your foot on Dennis' neck, and if he does something wrong, bring him right back to jail!"

Orlando says guys were like, *What the?... What type of prayer is that?* You didn't even hear an "Amen." Guys didn't know how to respond. Dennis said thanks and walked away. He must have been thinking the same as everyone else.

Point being: Guys need a sense of responsibility. A group of us were reminiscing about this recently—and laughing—Orlando told us about a book he'd read by Margaret Thatcher, former Prime Minister of the United Kingdom. At the height of global struggles during the Cold War, someone asked her, "Do you think you are a powerful leader?"

She replied, "Being a powerful leader is like being a woman; if you have to tell people that you are, then you're not." What wisdom in that answer! If you're powerfully leading, that action speaks for itself. You don't need to say it. Just like she doesn't need to walk into a room and announce, "I'm a woman." Everyone can see it.

You hear these guys in prison all the time saying, "I'm a grown-ass man! Don't tell me what to do." Well, if you were a grown-ass man, no one would have to tell you what to do. You'd just be doing it. Like the Bible says, when you see fruit, then you know the tree.

It's really this simple: Freedom isn't just doing what I want to do, it's doing what's right. The guys who get out of prison and function, they did the right things *while in prison*. Jesus said to the people who believed in Him, "You are truly my disciples if you remain faithful to my teachings. And you will know the truth, and the truth will set you free." While we were incarcerated, we were free to do the right thing.

This is a truth I discovered in 1986 when I came to faith in Jesus Christ: *If the Son sets you free, you will be free indeed!* There are two sides to this freedom in Jesus—what you are freed *from* and what you are freed *to*.

As a believer, you are freed *from* captivity to sin. The very definition of captivity is being confined. Apart from Jesus, we are bound in the impulses of sin. This doesn't necessarily mean you are living a wild lifestyle. It simply means that the primary authority in your life is your sinful nature. *It* is in control. *Sin* holds you captive. When you are born again, something beautiful happens—God gives you a new nature, filling you with His Holy Spirit and freeing you from this captivity. As the Apostle Paul says in 2 Corinthians 3:17: "where the Spirit of the Lord is, there is freedom."

In Christ, you are freed *to* live. This is about capacity—Jesus expands your capacity to live in relationship with your Heavenly Father. The bonds of sin broken, you are free *to* love, free *to* experience peace and joy, free *to* forgive and free *to* enjoy life to the fullest. As Jesus said in John 10:10: "I came that they may have life and have it abundantly."

This is true no matter who you are or what you've done.

Ephesians 2:10 says, "For we are his workmanship, created in Christ Jesus for good works, which God prepared beforehand." Perhaps you remember the great evangelist Billy Graham's famous words: "God loves you, and He has a wonderful plan for your life." His plan for your life is not burdensome—it's a blessing! It's not a checklist of do's and don'ts—it's an invitation: "Come to me, all you who are weary and burdened," and you are promised, "I will give you rest."

In the dictionary, *freedom* is defined as the power or right to act, speak or think without hindrance or restraint. That definition encompasses everything Jesus Christ has done for you. There is only one thing left for you to do—*live*.

And these guys—my band of brothers from other mothers—they're living proof of this good news.

CHAPTER 10

GETTING THE BAND BACK TOGETHER

Not long ago, we got together over a cool fall weekend in eastern PA—Orlando, Hammer and I all made our way to Rob's place. Darin joined us. As I've shared, my friend Rob is an amazing host. He spoiled us with comfort ... and lots of comfort food. (Let's see—we nearly burned the place down when Rob's gas grill caught fire; then I baptized Darin's laptop with a cup of coffee; Hammer brought his drone, and we stalked herds of deer and flocks of wild turkeys all over Rob's property, taking some amazing photographs; and lastly, we nearly got hypothermia climbing out of the heated swimming pool to towel off in near-freezing temps. What memories!)

One of the real blessings of the gathering was that we wound up talking about how each of us came to faith. Each of our roads is unique.

I shared my path to salvation in *Unshackled*, of course. It was quite a journey.

From my earliest childhood memories is Immaculate Conception Grade School and some really terrifying nuns ... visiting a confessional and saying "Hail Mary" to the Protestant Sunday School class Mom found for us, where my brother, Mike, and I perfected the art of escaping custody—would have made a young Jik the Barber proud!

There's the confusion of my alcoholic father dragging our family to church on Sunday mornings and then to the local tavern to watch him drink the afternoon away ... to the positive impression my childhood friend Bill and his family's Christianity had on me.

From seeing my stepfather, Loren, rise very early each morning and read from the well-worn pages of his old Bible to the time when a letter I'd written from prison and addressed to my brother in Pennsylvania wound up in the hands of a pastor's wife in Michigan, and her gracious response.

From a fellow inmate nicknamed Big Moses, rising early and shouting down the range, "Get up, you convicts, and praise the Lord! This is the day the Lord has made!" to his becoming my friend—and posting up outside my cell one morning when I'd gotten high, asking, "What are you doing, man?"

From an invitation to attend *Prison Invasion '86* and an outreach volunteer sharing his story of alcoholism with me in the yard to the most challenging words I'd ever heard: "Real men make commitments."

I wrote this in *Unshackled*: A long time ago, someone a lot smarter than me referred to our God as the Hound of Heaven. It's a strange title, I know. But I've personally experienced the tenacity with which God's love pursues—it's my story.

God's tenacious, pursuing love is written into all our stories. Even yours.

Orlando's faith story starts when he was a child, and it's especially meaningful to me because I was there, years later, to witness his faith-awakening.

He grew up Catholic, in a family of Catholics. He went to Catholic School from kindergarten to ninth grade. He will tell you that, in his mind, by that point he'd had about as much faith as he could handle. When he got locked up, he wasn't interested in church or any of the religious programs. But he was religiously curious. He looked into Buddhism and other faiths, never to the point of practicing, but just exploring different beliefs and their value. He will tell you he was *seeking*.

I'll tell you too: the Hound of Heaven was after Orlando! He wound up with Louie as a cellie for a time. Louie was an SWJ—a Servant With Jesus— someone who serves on a sort of board of deacons that our chaplain hand-selects to help with church activities like passing out hymnals, greeting and shaking hands, praying and helping with altar ministry, baptism, communion and such. Louie tried to share his faith with his cellie as often as opportunity presented itself.

Fast forward a couple years, Orlando wound up in E BLOCK, where I was. We had some mutual friends, so while we weren't really close, we were acquainted. One evening, pretty much out of the blue, he walked by my cell and saw that I was watching *Dateline NBC*—it happened to be a show about the four gospels. He stopped by my door for a minute, caught what was on TV and said something like, "If you've read one, you've read them all. What's the difference?"

We had a little dialogue—I don't really remember exactly what we said, but I tried to be courteous and not come across as argumentative or pushy. That was it.

A day or two later, he came back and asked me, "Do you have a Bible I could get?" I did, and I handed it right over. He asked, "What should I read?"

"Philippians" is what I told him.

People have asked me since, "Why did you say Philippians?" and the answer is simple: Philippians depicts Jesus as a servant. It's hard to argue with someone who came to serve you. I knew Orlando had some spiritual background. I didn't want to push him. I wanted Jesus to reveal Himself.

Orlando will tell you he was pretty self-conscious about it. He was wearing a jacket and tucked the Bible up under it as he walked back to his cell, so no one would see it. He waited until his cellie, Frank, went to sleep—Frank was on the bottom bunk, Orlando on the top—before he pulled it out. He read the first chapter of Philippians, broke down in tears ... and prayed.

The next day, he came back to my cell and said, "I got saved last night. I prayed, 'Lord Jesus, save me! I'm a nut.'" I giggled when he said it. He then asked, "Why are you laughing at me?" I assured him I wasn't laughing at him. I was rejoicing! His prayer was so refreshing to me. His was such an honest and effectual prayer!

And it only needs to be that simple—we tend to make things so complicated, so difficult and convoluted. Coming to faith is not some long, drawn-out process. There's no magic formula or fancy words. You don't even need a deep understanding of what's going on. It's just a matter of the heart: *You're God. I'm not. Help me, Lord!*

Over the next month or so we read a chapter a day together. We started through Genesis. And the interesting thing is that you weren't allowed in other guys' cells at that time. We spent probably two hours each night reading and talking through the Scriptures together. COs would come by and say, "Hey guys, you know you're not supposed to …" and they'd see what we were doing and be like, "… Okay" and walk on. We even had one CO who would sit down and join our conversation. We both remember, he'd pray with us—keeping his eyes open while we prayed. We understood. (I think that CO actually became a pastor.) The Lord blessed us. We had favor.

One of Orlando's early struggles in his faith was vulnerability. It's especially hard in prison, a place where you want to come across as anything but vulnerable. Presenting a tough exterior can feel like a matter of self-preservation, keeping people at arm's length, establishing distance. Being vulnerable means being transparent, letting people get close, and that's a hard transition to make in a prison environment.

I remember a time when he received a very painful letter from his daughter—*You ruined my life getting locked up* sort of stuff. He shared the letter with me. That sense of vulnerability is what I'm talking about; it's an opportunity to either take responsibility or to make excuses, to own it or to blame-shift. Healing begins with real transparency and ownership. We cried together. We prayed.

I'm so grateful for my friend Orlando. I'm proud of him. You know, once he gave me a Father's Day card, referring to me as a father-in-the-faith to him. I'm honored … and humbled. He is every bit the encouragement to me that I've ever been to him.

Hammer's story of coming to faith, too, is a winding road. He was born into a Protestant family, going to Sunday School and church as a young child. When he was eight years old, his parents divorced. He went to live with his father, and it was at that point they pretty much quit going to church.

He recalls a Sunday morning—he was maybe 11 or 12—there was a knock on their front door. It was a Christian evangelist, ministering door-to-door. "My dad invited him in and called me out of my room," Hammer recalls. "Dad explained to the man that we had gone to church in the past, but we'd sort of fallen away." This man shared the Gospel with them and, father and son, said the sinner's prayer. "We went to church for a while after that," he says, "but once I got into my teens, I got away from it again."

Hammer will tell you that he pretty much always believed, but it wasn't until he was in prison that it became real to him. "I saw lifers who were believers," he says. "Guys like Henry and Gene. I saw the way they acted, the way they behaved, and it really spoke to me. I had an expectation of getting out one day. These guys, they had no hope of getting out, and yet, this is the way they were. It was an eye-opener." Hammer says it was about this time that he made a decision to revisit, and to get serious, about his faith.

"Up to that point, I'd surrounded myself with the wrong people, the wrong influences. I wanted the genuine faith these guys had. I decided they were the type of people who could help me and would encourage me in my faith."

What drew me to Hammer, initially, was that he was a guy who was stable in his attitude and consistently polite toward everyone. Both inmates and officers. He never carried a chip around on his shoulder. I respected him, then and now.

What connected us was our mutual friendship with Henry, and our workouts together. These were no ordinary workouts, mind you. While Henry led us in plyometrics, I led our weight training. Hammer was the running coach. He excelled in endurance running and sprints. We would do these intense workouts for nearly the full 90 minutes of the scheduled yard out. Many guys attempted to join us, but they'd never return after their first experience—like

Johnny, who, half-way through, we found puking behind the bleachers. We had a saying when someone would give up: "Ring the bell!" Can't cut it? Go on, ring the bell!

Hammer is a real gentleman with a great sense of humor. And he is fun to be around. It didn't hurt that, through hard work, he'd risen to the top position in the kitchen, working with the culinary director. It meant he was an inmate privileged with plenty of extras when it came time to eat. Never a bad thing to have friends in high places!

Although he wasn't able to join us for this gathering at Rob's, Raffy is a beloved member of our reunion crew. He was my cellie for a brief time, and Orlando's. His testimony came up in our conversation—somebody was like, "What about Raffy's testimony? Wasn't there something about a witch doctor and a chicken?..."

Before Raffy got saved, he was visiting family in Puerto Rico and wound up going to a Santeria service. A witch doctor cut the head off a chicken and sprinkled its blood, mixed with alcohol, over Raffy's head. Then the man told Raffy, "When you get back to Philly, you're going to break up with your girlfriend and go to prison for a long time."

Seven years went by. All the while, Raffy and his cousin were dealing drugs. And theirs was a lucrative business. One evening, while posting up on a corner, Raffy spotted a van with tinted windows across the street. He warned his cousin, "That's the cops!" His cousin continued to hustle, but Raffy didn't sell a thing that night. The cops busted him anyhow.

People wonder if there is power in witchcraft. There is, but it's a power that oppresses. Thank God, Raffy's story doesn't end there. Two months after his arrest, sitting in a cell at the old Graterford Prison, Raffy saw his cellie pull out a Bible and start reading. Feeling pretty alone and lost, Raffy started reading the Bible each day like his cellie. He noticed that reading the Word of God brought him comfort and peace.

Not long after that, he was transferred to Rockview. There he met Orlando and me and started joining us for weekly services. Raffy dedicated his life to the Lord. I'm thrilled to call him both a friend and my brother in Christ!

Rob wasn't an inmate, but I feel as though he did my time with me. I first met him back in 1986, right after I'd become a believer. He was attending the church Larry pastored. Larry asked him if he'd be willing to visit a prisoner, saying, "I think he would really get along well with you."

Rob asked, "What's he in for?"

"Murder," Larry told him. "He's a lifer." Rob, who will tell you he hesitated initially for a moment, has been one of my dearest friends now, for 35-plus years.

He and I shared in one of the most poignant experiences I had while I was incarcerated. It was Christmas of 1988, at SCI Camp Hill. Rob was among a small group of guys who joined Larry in delivering Christmas care packages to all the inmates—gifts of socks and candy bars, as I remember. This time, the guests were allowed to come back into the cell blocks, to walk down the range, visiting men locked in their cells. It was unheard of; civilians just weren't allowed access back there. Rob and I have reminisced about it since—it was a very difficult experience for us both.

It was humbling for me. Until that point, the setting for our meetings had always been the safe confines of the visitation room. A neutral, dare I say somewhat-normal-feeling, setting with comfortable seating and vending machines. Without shackles or bars. Although I was a prisoner, it still sort of felt like we were peers, sitting and chatting. In this cell-block setting, however, I felt like a prisoner. He'd see me behind bars.

For his part, he remembers walking down the ground-floor tier, knowing he was on my block. He says it felt like Alcatraz to him, or like a scene in a movie. He saw Warner first.

As they spoke, I recognized Rob's voice—I knew he was coming and would see me next. I got really emotional even before I saw him.

When our eyes met, he says it was like a Hannibal Lector moment for him. "I saw my friend, Gene, standing there like a caged animal." We both began to weep. Bars are real, and they are unforgiving. It was very tough for us both. Perhaps that's one reason why we cherish spending time together today; we both know firsthand how miraculous God's power to deliver really is.

Rob's road to faith, like so many of ours, was long and winding as well. Although his family wasn't particularly devout, his childhood recollections include Sunday School and church. He earned perfect attendance pins and awards. His family moved to Harrisburg when he was 13.

One day, his mom slipped and fell on the ice and hurt her back. She looked in the telephone book for a chiropractor and came across Dr. Jack Heard. She was impressed that his yellow-pages ad read "If there's no answer at the office, call the doctor's residence," and included his home number.

Jack was a Christian and had a powerful ministry. He'd led thousands to Christ, no exaggeration. Add Rob's mom to the list; she got powerfully saved. A couple of years later, his dad got saved too. Rob remembers, when he was about 16 or so, his parents said he needed to go to church with them and began penalizing him if he didn't—taking his car away, things like that. Then came his turn; he went to a Full Gospel meeting and heard Jack speak. Today he says, "God pricked my heart that day." He went forward and said the sinner's prayer, and he knew something had happened—something felt different.

But he had no Christian friends, no real positive peer influence in his life. He fell into the usual teenager stuff and shuffled his faith experience to the backburner.

A few years passed. He was in college, living the college-student experience, when he had a real Christ-encounter.

"I was driving down Market Street in Mechanicsburg, sunroof open," he recalls, "and I heard the Lord's voice. 'Who are you going to serve? You or Me?'" Rob went to see Jack Heard. Jack took him down into his basement to talk and pray, and Rob was baptized in the Holy Spirit.

He asked Jack, "What now?"

Jack told him, "You get into a Bible study and join a men's discipleship group. Now, you grow in your relationship with God." It set the pattern for the rest of his life.

Darin shared his story with us. In his earliest recollections, his parents sent him to a little Christian school for two years of pre-kindergarten. He was the star of his pre-school's annual Christmas pageant ... literally, he was an actual star, in a costume made of cardboard and covered with aluminum foil to reflect light over the manger. The rest of his childhood wasn't very religious, and he, too, grew through all the typical adolescent struggles. At 16, encountering more serious teenage scrapes, he was invited to spend a weekend with his older brother, whom he idolized. This brother had recently come to faith in Jesus—so this invite was loaded.

"He planned a weekend fishing trip for us," Darin says, "on Lake Jessop." At the time, this lake along the St. John's River was known for being the most alligator-populated body of water in Florida. "We got in this tiny two-person boat, and my brother rowed us out into the midst of a bunch of gators." He can still describe the way alligator eyes and nostrils were visible all around them. "My brother opened up his tackle-box, pulled out a Bible and said, 'I want to talk to you about Jesus Christ. And if you don't want to hear it, you can swim for shore.'"

His brother walked him through the Gospel—the Good News: God loves you. He sent His Son, Jesus Christ, to take on the penalty for all your sins and shortcomings. If you believe that Jesus is who He says He is and has done what He says He's done, Jesus' perfection pays that price for you, reconciling you to God.

Darin explained that as he listened to his brother share, the thing that hit him between the eyes was the word *perfect*—to go to heaven when you die, you must be perfect.

"Not just good, but perfect," he explained. Darin's belief up to that point was that good people—people who aren't bad people—would go to heaven when they died. But that word *perfect* got his attention. Darin says he knew in his heart that he wasn't perfect, not even to his own standards, let alone God's. He put his faith in Jesus that day, surrounded by alligators.

That Hound of Heaven—He just keeps loving, keeps pursuing. He uses life's circumstances and situations; sends people to pray and to preach; seizes opportunities to reveal Himself and His love through others. Little glimpses here and there, at first. Challenges. Reminders. Invitations.

And none of it is coincidence.

Warner—you remember, Big Moses—tells the story of his coming to faith. It was Easter Sunday in 1979. Up to that point in his life, he was living, as he says, "Without conscience or fear of God." A guy named Ted arrived to do his time at Camp Hill. Warner passed him on the walk one day and said, "How's it going?"

Ted quickly turned their conversation to Jesus, to which Warner replied, "I don't believe in God."

"Well, Jesus loves you," Ted said.

This guy pursued Warner. Every time they'd bump into each other, Ted would start in praying and preaching. Nowhere was off limits for what was on his heart. And Warner couldn't get away, couldn't hide. He'd walk out in the rec yard, and here comes Ted. Chow line, same. And always the same thing: "Jesus loves you, Warner."

One day they started talking about heaven and hell. Warner said, "Well, hell it is!"

Right then and there, Ted dropped to his knees, started crying and prayed out loud, "Jesus, save his soul!"

Warner didn't understand what was happening, so he grabbed him under his arms to pull him to his feet. "Man, you can't do that here. This isn't the kind of place where you want to show weakness."

Ted wasn't fazed. He wasn't deterred. There were several occasions like this; the guy refused to give up.

Warner recognized there was something different about this guy, though. There was something genuine and authentic about Ted's faith. No matter how much he'd argue, how much he fussed, this guy just kept coming back, kept reminding Warner, "Jesus loves you."

"Two months into this, the Holy Spirit began to trouble my thoughts," Warner says. "I became absorbed with who Jesus is. His light began penetrating my darkness. Things around me became dim and vague. And, around every turn, here comes Ted asking, 'You get saved yet?'"

Easter Sunday, they had a sunrise service in the main yard. Warner was invited to check it out. They had some trumpets and trombones playing. Somebody was strumming a guitar; they were singing resurrection songs. Warner says he fell under heavy conviction about the weight of his sin ... and who Jesus is. "The Holy Spirit was, at once, both convicting me and convincing me that Jesus Christ is Lord and Savior; that He is the Good Shepherd."

That night, alone in his cell, Warner prayed, "Jesus, forgive my sins. Save me from the wretchedness and give me this new and abundant life that You promise." He knew something had happened. Something had changed inside. He fell asleep that night in total peace—for the first time in his entire life.

The next day Ted came by, doing his thing: "Jesus loves you. Did you get saved yet?" This time, Warner told him he'd accepted Jesus into his life. So used to his refusals, Ted missed his answer altogether. Warner had to say it a few times before it set in. Ted started crying again, and this time Warner joined him—they shed tears of joy.

Warner, himself, became a vessel the Hound of Heaven used in my own life—and in so many of our lives.

Last year, Big Moses had his sentence reduced by a York County judge from life without parole to 50 years to life. I still feel it's unfair. But he's closing in on 50 years—I can't wait for the day he wakes up in my guest room ... and I wake up to hear his voice ringing through the house, "O Victory in Jesus, My Savior forever! He sought me and bought me, with His redeeming blood!"

But in the meantime, his ministry continues to bear tremendous fruit. He lives each day to share Christ as our only hope. His life testifies: he never "speak[s] of being in need, for [he has] learned in whatever situation [he's in] to be content" (Philippians 4:11). He serves as an example of what it looks like to follow after Jesus—what it looks like to love God and love others.

Big Moses calls me each week from Rockview. Before he even says a word, I can feel his enthusiasm through the phone. His greeting is like an infusion of holy joy: victory has been won over a dark enemy. "Gene-eeeeee! Praise the Lord!"

His laughter takes me right back to those early morning declarations down the range, "Wake up, men! This is the day the Lord has made!" The purpose for his every call is to bless and encourage me. He always does.

—————

These guys are family to me. When we gather it's a reunion, not unlike when you gather with your loved ones. "Do you remember when me and Henry...?" and "How about that time when...?" and "What do you suppose ever became of...?" And laughter? Oh my! Laughing together to the point of tears!

This particular weekend at Rob's, we must have gotten to the bottom of a pot of coffee. Orlando said, "Who's got a stinger?"

Orlando, Hammer and I laughed. Rob and Darin were like, "Huh?"

A stinger is an inmate staple—an extension cord with paper clips jammed in the female end and used to boil water for coffee or, more often in our case, to make *chichis*. You'd take a potato chip bag, clean it out and fill it up with water—maybe a pinch of salt to help it boil. You put some ramen noodles in, some seasoning, drop a stinger in and in a minute or two you'd hear that bag start motorboating. *Soup's on!* Guys would get creative; fashion themselves real cell-block culinarians.

I don't want to brag, but I got pretty creative. Onions, green peppers, extra leftovers, seasonings—I did mention how good it was to have friends in high places, like Hammer in the kitchen.

But stinger technology wasn't fool proof. Just about once a day, somebody's stinger would short out and trip the breaker, killing power to a whole row of cells down the range. It was bad if you caused it, because you'd just killed everyone's televisions and radios. Guys would be like, "Who's got the stinger?" *Uh ... that would be me. Oops!*

Guards would come take your stinger and your supplies, and you'd be embarrassed that you caused the blackout. Staff could write you up, but everybody knew me. I just endured a little teasing. Worst part for me was that this meal was going to be great—I had filled a *huge* chip bag with ramen and rice, added in tons of kitchen goodies. Man, it was bubbling away, smelling awesome. All I can figure is that something must have shifted inside the bag and the paperclip leads touched, and ... *POP*!

This opened the floor for several chichi and stinger recollections. One of Orlando's first stinger experiences, for instance: he reached in to test the temperature of the water ... failing to realize he was leaning on a metal chair. *ZAP!*

Someone recalled, "What about the time Louie made that chichi he was so proud of, boasting he'd added five seasoning packets?" *We all remembered!* It was so salty it brought tears to our eyes.

Speaking of things that bring tears to your eyes, someone asked, "What was Brian's cellie's name?" Everyone knew immediately where this recollection was going.

For a season inside, I lived directly across the range from a cell that just reeked. No kidding, you walked too close to the cell and the odor would overwhelm you. Halting. Choking. You'd double over, fighting off the urge to vomit. A guy we knew, Brian, got assigned to share the stinky cell.

I walked over one day—I'd tied a t-shirt around my nose, but it didn't help—and asked, "Brian, what is that stench?" Brian slid the bag out from under his bunkie's bed and showed me: his cellie had a laundry bag full of brown prison-issue socks, each as stiff as cardboard. Instinctively, I backed away. "Man! You need to throw those out!"

His cellie—whose name now escapes us, but whose body odor still lingers—seemed like just an average guy quietly doing his time, but he refused to launder his socks. *Never!* No exaggeration, at the end of a day, or week, or however often, he'd pull the sweat-fouled socks off his feet and toss them into this bag, fishing out a previously worn pair to replace them. I don't know how Brian did it, living in that cloud of stink.

And then, there are those recollections that bring heartfelt tears. Someone asked, "Do you guys remember Mikey Smith?"

That family thing I'm talking about was never so evident as when tragedy struck. Mikey was a good guy, maybe in his 40s. Everyone knew him and liked him. He was diagnosed with pancreatic cancer, and we all knew that that meant; his was now a death sentence.

One by one, we shared recollections. Guys went over to the infirmary to help him cut up his food; Warner would go over and sing to comfort him. Right near the end, they moved Mikey into hospice care. We recalled gathering in Chap's office and talking to his sister on the telephone—it was a very moving experience then. Still is now, looking back.

Family.

CHAPTER 11

SCI PHOENIX

Walking through the doors at SCI Phoenix was emotional for me. I was filled with wonder and awe. This is really unheard of, a former inmate, a lifer, having the opportunity to come in as a free man and share his testimony with these men.

But even beyond that, the privilege of helping others discover God's love for them, to help them realize their identity and purpose is in Him, is overwhelming. It's like my friend Will always says, "You can't make this stuff up!"

Will—"Surf," as we call him—has been a valuable friend to walk with over the years. Even more so today, as we serve in ministry in different locations. I could never have imagined his lifelong commitment to Christ that Sunday morning we first met. I was on my way to chapel when I saw him sitting on a trash can down on the end of D BLOCK, and I said, "Good morning! You want to come to church with me?" He politely declined, and this became our Sunday morning ritual for several weeks in a row.

Talking to Surf, I noticed he was dealing with some painfully dry skin. One Sunday when I saw him, I dropped off a bottle of lotion I bought at the commissary for him. Prison culture often misinterprets kindness. People give you stuff, they expect something in return. In fact, I'd given guys stuff over the years—sneakers, food, lotion, whatever—I always had to assure them I was just being a friend. No strings attached. Surf will tell you, a white guy noticing a black man's skin and caring enough to buy him some lotion ... he wondered if I was gay.

One day, I looked up to see Surf walking into our Sunday School class. He sat down way in the back. He was writing letters or something, not really paying attention. That was fine with me.

A couple weeks later, he moved a little closer. He was still writing, not participating. But then, he came a little closer still. Next thing I knew, Surf was sitting in the front row, a Bible open on his lap, participating. God is good!

I'm so proud of him today. I marvel at his devotion to bettering himself as a man and a minister. He went to work on his education, earning a degree through Villanova University in the Spring of 2020. I pray for Surf each morning, praying specifically for the commutation of his life sentence. Should the Lord open the door, I've got a room prepared for my brother here in Fort Worth.

What's it like walking into a prison for me today? Well, I *know* prisons. I feel pretty confident walking in because I can read the officers, I can read the inmates, and I can read the culture. The people I meet and speak with don't recognize, at first, that I can see and understand all this. I also know the guys appreciate that someone has come in to speak to them—we always appreciated guests visiting. And I know that my testimony is going to connect. I've been there, in their seats, in their skin. So, I'm excited. I know God is at work.

And of SCI Phoenix specifically, Rob and I had gone to SCI Graterford a year or so prior, where Surf had been housed—that was the last time I'd seen him. Graterford was an older prison, so not long after I'd visited, they shut it down and transferred the men to SCI Phoenix, built right next door. While this was my first visit to this new facility, most of the staff and inmates were the same men I'd met previously. As some 200 or so men filed into the auditorium, several remembered me from the Graterford visit. I recognized a few of them.

My opening comments are never rehearsed, and that morning in front of the men at SCI Phoenix was no different. I began with a testimony—

Not long ago, I was invited to speak to an auditorium holding a thousand students on the campus of Christ for the Nations International (CFNI) in Dallas, Texas. These students there are all devoted Christians, training for a life in ministry. They didn't need any coaxing to worship God with reckless abandon—they were fully engaged with singing and shouting hallelujahs for a good 45 minutes before I was introduced. Praise filled the auditorium. The Lord's presence was palpable in the place.

As I began to speak, I felt a nudge to share about how one day, 15 or so years prior to my release from prison, I was reading my Bible in my cell and the Holy Spirit told me to write down three things I *liked* about my dad; three qualities of his that I *admired*.

I immediately felt uncomfortable. Mad uncomfortable. I tried to avoid the question and move on with reading the chapter before me, but the Lord wouldn't let me off so easy. I struggled, protesting in my heart; I couldn't possibly think of qualities of his I liked or admired. Dad divorced Mom when I was six. He drank himself to death at 51. My memories and recollections of him include his showing up at my school and sporting events drunk and embarrassing me. I didn't have much to work with. *Let's see ... when Mom really needed him ... he showed up with beer.*

The Lord pressed me: *Write down three things.* I took up a pen and paper. Felt like it took me forever, but I eventually scratched out the following:
   1. He dressed well.
   2. He kept his car clean.
   3. He taught me to run ahead and open doors for my mother and my sister.

As I read over what I'd written, I felt pretty good about it. He dressed well. Nothing fancy, but he always managed to tuck in his shirt and keep his shoes shined. He kept his car clean. There were so many areas of his life where he was irresponsible, but he took care of the car.

And he taught me to always be a gentleman where opening doors was concerned.

These three things were all true of my dad. And I realized, in that instant, they'd made an impression on me. I see those glimpses of him ... in me. And I appreciated that.

While I sat there looking at my list through tear-filled eyes, the Holy Spirit said, "Now you can stop complaining about your dad."

No matter how our earthly fathers treated us or abdicated their responsibilities, we have a Heavenly Father who never fails us, and who never stops loving us.

When I finished speaking that day, there was an altar call of sorts—a chance for students to come forward for prayer. Several came forward, I'd guess maybe a hundred or so. I prayed over them, and then someone in charge told the students they were free to leave or they could stay if they'd like to talk and fellowship a bit longer. Worship music played on. The Lord had really stirred a lot of their hearts. I made my way around the room, meeting, hugging and praying with students. I spoke the Lord's purpose over them and affirmed His work in their lives. Eventually, after maybe a half-hour or so, the room began to clear. I was unable to leave, myself. I didn't know what to do, I just knew I couldn't leave yet. I sat down in the front row.

A student with a leather shoulder bag approached, introduced himself and sat down next to me. "Thank you for sharing your story," he said, "especially the part about your dad." I could tell he was fighting back his emotions as he asked, "Can I show you something?" He reached into his bag and pulled out a workbook with the word 'Mentoring' printed boldly on the cover. He began thumbing through its pages. I noticed right away how well-worn this workbook was, each page containing handwritten notes, underlines and highlights.

He found the page he was looking for, folded it over and looked down at the floor. "I've nearly completed the book," he said. "I've answered all the questions except one. There's one I couldn't answer." He pointed to the question and handed me the workbook. It read: *Describe a few characteristics that you like about your dad.*

Tears filled my eyes as this student said, "Now I know how to answer it." We prayed and cried together. The Holy Spirit confirmed, right then, why I was unable to leave.

As I shared this story at SCI Phoenix, it really connected. Sometimes when I'm speaking, this sort of thing happens—I hadn't gone in planning to mention this—in fact I hadn't even considered it. Yet, as I started to speak, the story flooded out of me. A God thing.

The men sat in silence, eyes fixed on me, and several were visibly moved. So many of these men, like me—like a lot of us—needed to address father-wounds, issues that have caused them deep injuries, abiding hurt, resentment and anger. If we let Him, our Heavenly Father breaks the shackles. He heals our wounds. He is the Lord of *life beyond.*

For the next 45 minutes or so, I shared other parts of my testimony—my crime, drug abuse to mask my shame and guilt, years of rebellion and then some of the many sign-posts God planted in my life. I shared of my salvation and years of discipleship, and the difficulty of all those attempts for commutation denied by the Pennsylvania Board of Pardons.

I was very mindful of the truth from God's Word, that He had placed me where I was at that very moment. Here I was, standing before my peers—men I knew. Men whose hurts and whose need for Jesus I'd known personally.

I shared how being teachable and correctable are two things I make a priority in my daily walk. Being teachable ensures my spiritual growth. Being correctable, no matter how far I get off track, offers me the ability to get back on course toward my destiny within God's Kingdom.

"Nobody likes a know-it-all," I told them, "but for a lot of years I was that guy. I would say, 'I know! I know!' when someone was trying to teach me. I was insecure and defensive, not wanting to look ignorant or weak in anyone's eyes. It was pride and insecurity."

There is an unmistakable arrogance in being unteachable. It's an attitude that will always be destructive. Freedom comes in the form of God's grace—freedom to admit that, no matter how mature you are, there is always room for growth.

Sharing principles about surrendering, being teachable and correctible and serving others with inmates is pretty hardcore because of the strong bravado mentality in prison. Like Orlando's testimony, that vulnerability is something you avoid in keeping your guard up. The prison atmosphere is permeated with defiance to prove some form of bravery or to impress others. It was my rebellious nature, my arrogance, during the early years of incarceration that earned me 23 misconducts. Mostly insolence: I'd rear up and mouth off to authority simply because I had a total disregard for others. All that mattered to me was me.

I quoted Philippians 2:5-9 (NIV): "In your relationships with one another, have the same mindset as Christ Jesus: Who, being in very nature God, did not consider equality with God something to be used to his own advantage; rather, he made himself nothing by taking the very nature of a servant, being made in human likeness. And being found in appearance as a man, he humbled himself by becoming obedient to death—even death of a cross! Therefore God exalted him to the highest place and gave him the name that is above every name."

This attitude that Jesus had was that of a servant. I was so excited sharing this with the guys—this passage has been so influential for me personally and in my ministry. If Jesus, while remaining God, became a servant, then I want to be a servant too. It is so prevalent in the Bible: Moses is called a servant of the Lord 40 times; Joshua is called a servant; Paul calls himself a servant many times—I want to be identified with men like these.

I shared that I'd looked the word "servant" up in the dictionary and asked myself, *Do I really want to be someone who performs duties for others?* Many guys laughed.

Then I told them the two main characteristics of being a servant are *having no rights* and *considering others more important than yourself.* A handful of guys laughed.

Then I told them that Jesus gave up all His rights to do the will of the Father, even to the point of death, and that He did this because He considered others' needs more important than His own comfort and convenience. Because of this attitude, God exalted Him to the highest place and gave Him the name that is above all others. No one laughed now.

By this name, Jesus, many would experience freedom from death and the bondage of sin.

In closing, I talked about how important it is for men to get to know God as our Heavenly Father, through Jesus Christ our Savior. Choosing to become a student of the Word helps us discover our new identity as a child of God and the wonder and awe of God as our Father.

The lion's share of men in prison come from broken homes with abusive or irresponsible fathers. I get it. I get their hurt. My father abdicated his responsibilities, leaving me with a very flawed view of God as my Father. But when I stopped viewing God through the murky lens of my earthly father, and allowed the Bible to accurately define Him instead, I discovered a very faithful and loving Father. This permitted me to feel loved apart from performance and to know and have confidence in Him, without the fear of rejection.

I told them, "That day at SCI Rockview when God said, 'Write down three things you like about your dad,' it was an invitation for me to experience a new level of freedom I badly needed. And this is your invitation."

The excitement I felt walking into SCI Phoenix to share with the men that day was matched with heartache as I left. Leaving guys whom I have come to love as brothers behind is never easy. I knew where I was headed when I walked out, and I know all too well what awaited these men when it was time to leave the chapel area and head back into their cell block, with all the rules and routines. I pray for them, appealing to the God "who is able to do far more abundantly than all that we ask or think, according to the power at work within us" (Ephesians 3:20).

It's especially hard to walk away from Surf. I know he's in great hands, with a great ministry. I know that he is "God's workmanship, created in Christ Jesus for good works, which God prepared beforehand, that we should walk in them" (Ephesians 2:10). Still, I miss my brother.

The day after our visit, he sent me this email:

Great is the Lord, and greatly to be praised! I pray that this message finds you doing well. As for myself, I am still floating from yesterday's Worship service. There is no doubt that you posted something.

Just like before, it was surreal to see you again brother. There had been a buzz all week leading up to Sunday. Needless to say, that the Holy Spirit did not disappoint. The building was filled with over 200 men hungry for a word from one of our own. The room was electric, as you spoke with confidence and conviction. Words of encouragement flowed from your mouth like rivers of living water. Shouts of Yes! and Amen! filled the room as the men, and women were touched by your powerful words of faith and deliverance. I say women, because also in attendance were Jennifer, (she interprets for the deaf members of our congregation), Virginia, (my seminary school mentor), and Patty. Of course, you know that Patty and I had an instant connection. How does that always happen? Also attending was Alan, who is on the board of directors for our seminary school.

Rob did a great job of introducing You. He spoke about how he was not the speaker, just the one who was preparing the way. Rob set the table perfectly, and you served up the meal. It was a two-hankie day for me. I needed one to blow my nose, and another one to wipe the tears from my eyes, as I was continuously moved by Your testimony of God's awesome work in your life. It was humbling to hear a mighty man of God speak so highly of me during the course of the service. Thank goodness Patty was there to comfort me. As I listened to you speak, I thought about how blessed I was to have so many tremendous people in my life, many of whom I have met through you. Man, you shared so many things, but of particular interest to the men was your word that God is not a respecter of person. You wanted the men to know that God could do for them everything that He has done for you, and then some. Amen to that!

Mega-blessings 2 you,
Will

Not long after my SCI Phoenix visit, the world was turned on its ear.

My very first recollection of the COVID-19 virus was a news video from the street in China. There were people in white chemical bodysuits removing a lady from a vehicle. She appeared to be struggling, resisting even, until she collapsed on the street and lay motionless.

My thoughts ran wild—is this virus attacking people? Did the authorities removing her from a car at the intersection kill her? How did they come to know that this lady was infected so that they wore chemical gear and masks? There wasn't much information out at the time and, probably like many others, I figured this is happening in China, some 7,500 miles away from Fort Worth, Texas.

I recalled the H1N1 virus that swept through SCI Rockview in 2009. I remember the long lines that formed outside the infirmary—men shivering with fever and throwing up while they waited to be seen. Guys would be talking to you one minute and vomiting the next. It was really contagious and really terrible for those who caught it. Surprisingly, I never got sick.

But as word spread and concern grew over COVID, I began to take it a little more seriously. Like everyone else, I was trying my best to follow health guidelines, not touch things, especially my face. The hardest part for me was having to stop hugging and embracing everyone I met. No hugs, no more hand-shaking—it felt so strange, so wrong. So now it's the fist-bump or the elbow-tap? I went hybrid: fist-to-elbow.

I traveled to Pennsylvania in early March to conduct worship services in East Stroudsburg. The folks at the church were already practicing social-distancing (this was the weekend when mask-wearing, social-distancing and shutdowns were just starting to be implemented across the country). I stayed with Rob, and just about every time I turned around, he had me disinfect my hands.

By the time I landed back in Dallas-Fort Worth, things looked and felt very different. Our towns were shut down, and there was very little traffic on the roads. I stopped to pick up a few groceries and found the paper towel and toilet paper aisles bare. I smiled. Having been in prison, I'd learned to stock up on TP! No kidding—I'd trade cigarettes for extra rolls back in the day. Old habits are hard to shake; no TP crisis for me, I knew my cabinets at home were well stocked. (I counted when I got home: 72 rolls!)

Social-distancing was really awkward for me at first. *How do I stop interacting with family and friends?* As bars and restaurants were being closed for dining in, Babe's Chicken scrambled to facilitate takeout and curbside service. I witnessed the intense efforts and long hours put in by everyone to keep things afloat and to keep our employees working.

As chaplain, I am committed to serving the workers. I showed up and cheered them on. On a few occasions, there were opportunities for me to jump in and help answer phones, prep to-go bags or run errands. Our managers were like coaches, drawing up revisions to the game plan on the fly.

I walked in the back door of Babe's Frisco one day with my bandana wrapped around my face, and in my best Texas drawl I shouted, "Hey, hard workers! Ya'll so incredible."

Spotting the manager, I asked, "Hi, Erin, how's it going?"

She turned to see my mask—looking like an outlaw in an old western, I suppose—and commented, "Aren't you concerned about wearing a mask? You know, with your past?"

I totally missed that she was teasing. I was thinking, *I know some of our older managers with pre-existing health concerns were sent home for their own safety. And I did have a stroke a few years ago ...*

I spoke up, "You know, I'm feeling pretty healthy. I don't have any ..." Her humor hit me mid-sentence. She meant *with my history*. Everybody cracked up, and right when it seemed a moment of levity was just what everyone needed.

Truthfully, it does feel awkward walking into businesses with my face covered. I suppose that's true for all of us, though. Such strange times we're living through.

I'll tell you what made me most uncomfortable is the way so many of my normal activities were interrupted. I am a creature of habit and routines. A stay-at-home order took me back to 24-hour-a-day lockdowns in prison. You might not think there are liberties, comforts and privileges to be had in prison, but there are. Being confined to your cell for 24 hours a day—without showers, job assignments and school—forced to eat bologna sandwiches each night—no visits allowed, no phone calls, no worship services—is a horrible experience. I'd spend that time memorizing scripture, doing pushups (like 1,500 a day) and catching up on letters. But there was always an end in sight. Lockdowns might have lasted a couple days. It sucked, but you knew what you were in for, and for how long. With this pandemic, *who knows?...*

My ministry at Babe's moved from quantity to quality in that I was having more one-on-one conversations with managers and workers. Instead of walking into the restaurant where I would see dozens of workers busy with their responsibilities, I was only seeing a few at a time. This provided me the opportunity to speak more with them about their needs and how the virus was affecting them personally.

As I've said, Babe's is a family. A common concern was for co-workers who were part of the work furlough due to the closing of our dine-in business. Curbside and to-go business takes far fewer employees. There just wasn't work enough to keep the normal staff employed ... and managers were really feeling the weight of this. The Vinyard family was working day and night, making necessary adjustments with operations for Babe's to accommodate as many employees as possible. I took time to remind our managers that while Babe's is our resource, God is our Provider. And we can trust Him. Every morning for years, I've included in my prayers that as God provided Abraham a ram, He's provided me with a Lamb.

While I was working to comfort others, I had to safeguard my mind from the onslaught of fear bombarding us all through social media and the news. The crazier the reports, the more attention they seemed to garner. I decided to practice Isaiah 26:3: "You will keep him in perfect peace whose mind is stayed on you, because he trusts in you." Even as I'm writing these words, we're not out of the pandemic woods. But that Isaiah passage rings true. Lean into Him.

CHAPTER 12

THE STORY WE FIND OURSELVES IN

The most famous verse in the Bible says, "For God so loved the world, that he gave his only Son, that whoever believes in him should not perish but have eternal life" (John 3:16). This is the Gospel or *Good News* through which people discover God's love for them and come to enjoy a renewed relationship with Him. This Gospel message is an invitation to *you*.

The Bible declares that each and every one of us is born into a selfish state, inclined toward sin: "Behold, I was brought forth in iniquity, and in sin did my mother conceive me" (Psalm 51:5). Of our own choosing, we become prideful, ungrateful and resentful, neither fearing God nor knowing Him. An honest look in the mirror should be all you need to convince yourself of your humanness and shortcomings ... but, if not, the Apostle Paul paints a very clear, all-inclusive picture of mankind's condition: "None is righteous, no, not one; no one understands; no one seeks for God. All have turned aside; together they have become worthless; no one does good, not even one" (Romans 3:10-12).

The good news is, God's love doesn't leave us in that alienated state—He doesn't leave *you* in that alienated state. "The LORD looks down from heaven on the children of man, to see if there are any who understand, who seek after God" (Psalm 14:2-3). God's saving love is revealed to us in Jesus: "In this the love of God was made manifest among us, that God sent his only Son into the world, so that we might live through him" (1 John 4:9). How is this possible? Jesus "bore our sins in his body on the tree, that we might die to sin and live to righteousness. By his wounds you have been healed" (1 Peter 2:24).

Jesus' death on the cross demonstrates the degree to which *you* are deeply loved by God: "For one will scarcely die for a righteous person—though perhaps for a good person one would dare even to die—but God shows his love for us in that while we were still sinners, Christ died for us" (Romans 5:7-8).

That phrase, "while we were still sinners" is really important. Love like this cannot be earned; you can't become good enough or do enough good. The good news is *you don't have to.* You are already loved by God! The Hound of Heaven pursues your wounded, wandering heart with a loving invitation: "If you confess with your mouth that Jesus is Lord and believe in your heart that God raised him from the dead, you will be saved" (Romans 10:9).

Maybe you've never done this. If not, today is your day. "Behold, now is the favorable time; behold, now is the day of salvation" (2 Corinthians 6:2).

There's no secret handshake to learn, and no magic words or phrases to recite. Remember Orlando's prayer? "Jesus, save me! I'm a nut!" That sort of simple honesty, spoken from the heart, is a totally effectual prayer. God is alive—and He is listening to you!

Would you take this moment—yes, right now, while you're holding this book—to pray? If you don't know what to say, pray something like this, making it your own—

"Heavenly Father, I know that I have sinned and fall short of Your holiness. I believe that Jesus Christ is the Son of God, and that He died for my sins. I welcome Jesus to be Lord and Savior of my life. Amen."

Maybe you said a prayer like that years ago, but you've wandered away. There's no greater picture—no more emotional picture—of a father's love than we find in the parable of the prodigal son. You've probably heard the story recorded in the gospel of Luke:

A son chose to walk away from his father's love and blessing, cashed in his inheritance and set out to live life on his own terms, to live his way. In time, he realized the life he thought he wanted wasn't at all that he'd imagined. The party was over. Awakened to the reality that he'd made a mistake, the son longed for home. He set out, worried about the reception he would receive from his father the entire journey home. He planned to crawl back apologetically, pleading that maybe, just maybe, his father would let him come back, even if only to be a servant slopping his father's pigs. Perhaps you know that feeling—wishing you could go back, undo, re-do or somehow make something right?

Here's that beautiful picture: "But while [the son] was still a long way off, his father saw him and felt compassion, and ran and embraced him and kissed him. And the son said to him, 'Father, I have sinned against heaven and before you. I am no longer worthy to be called your son.' But the father said to his servants, 'Bring quickly the best robe, and put it on him, and put a ring on his hand, and shoes on his feet. And bring the fattened calf and kill it, and let us eat and celebrate. For this my son was dead, and is alive again; he was lost, and is found.' And they began to celebrate" (Luke 15:20-24).

If you're "out" there, having wandered, this is *your* invitation: *Come home!*

Maybe like Orlando, you grew up going to Catholic schools and, by your teenage years, figured you'd had all the religion you could handle. Maybe like him, you've spent time since searching after truth in different religious traditions and coming up empty.

Maybe like Hammer, you grew up in a church-going family, attending Sunday School as a child. Maybe you've always *sort of believed* in God, just never experienced a personal relationship with Him. I hope his testimony will encourage you; you can move beyond *sort-of faith* to a real, vibrant and growing relationship with Jesus.

Wherever you are, I can promise you this: You make hundreds if not thousands of decisions every day, yet none will be as powerful and life-changing as the decision to follow Jesus. I did it. My friends have also. God's love is real. He loves you, and so do I. If you've made a decision to follow Jesus, please reach out to me. I want to hear your story. I want to give thanks.

Hearing from people who've been challenged or encouraged by my story is such a blessing. As I shared earlier, I can never predict what the Lord will do with my testimony. In one instance, like with Big John grieving the loss of his sister, God used my story to touch his heart with healing and restoration. In another, an inmate in Michigan named Zach—a man I've never met—dropped me a note. A friend had sent Zach a copy of my book. He wrote: "I just wanted to thank you for sharing your story. There were parts that made me laugh, cry and even get a little angry at parts where only somebody else doing time can relate. Your book was a blessing to me and a little breath of fresh air that I needed." He went on to mention specifically what spoke encouragement to his heart: "You speak of something at the end of your book that I'm kind of relating to right now, that is the 'process,' as I believe you refer to it. When the Lord told you He was going to release you, and it took 20 months."

I don't believe in coincidences. That day I met Surf sitting on a trash can at the end of D BLOCK, or the time I saw Doc walk into chapel and announce, "Doc is in the house!"—I couldn't have known how the Lord would use those occasions so powerfully in their lives. I know it's not a coincidence when an inmate named Marcus, a Muslim, writes and says, "a copy of your book fell into my lap." Marcus wasn't looking for God, but God found him. He wrote that he remembered seeing his grandparents, who were Christians, "pray to God, read the Bible and be happy, not caring what other people thought. Just like Warner." I especially love that Warner's testimony spoke so powerfully to Marcus. I know my encounter with Big Moses was no coincidence. Neither was Marcus'.

Jodi, an inmate in Texas, had a similar encounter. She writes, "God led me to your book. Every time I walk into our spiritual library here on Crain Unit, I pray for Him to lead me to the book He wants me to read that particular week. He led me straight to yours."

Friend, I don't know how you came to hold this book in your hands. But I don't believe it happened by chance. However it is that you've come to read these words, in this moment, this is what I pray your heart will hear—

You are as unique as the writing of this book. Your uniqueness is seen in that God lovingly created you and breathed life into your lungs. He created you with a purpose no one else can fulfill. God desires for you to walk in relationship with Him, to worship Him and enjoy Him forever.

Each of us is unique. Each of our stories is unique. Yet, we all find ourselves together in one, overarching story—*His* story. And *life after* you've found yourself in His story is life truly worth living.

EPILOGUE

Whenever and wherever I've had the privilege to share, and in a majority of the letters I receive from people who've read *Unshackled*, people ask for updates. What's happening with Big Moses? Surf? What's happening with their cases? Do you ever hear anything about your cousin Bobby or stepbrother Sid? Here are some brief updates, keeping in mind—and giving thanks—that each of their stories, like mine and yours, continues to unfold.

Warner, aka Big Moses, is still ... *Big Moses*! We talk on the telephone each week. His calls are ministry, always about encouraging *me*, and they always hit the mark. His enthusiasm for what God is doing in and around him spills over into whatever my day holds. Warner's life sentence was amended, meaning he will be eligible for parole in the next few years. Until then, he rises every morning to sing of the Lord's faithfulness and to His glory.

As I mentioned, Surf has continued to further his education, even earning his college degree. He and I talk often. I'm praying with him for the commutation of his life sentence. In the meantime, he serves in chapel and has a vibrant ministry among the inmates at SCI Phoenix.

I am not in touch with my cousin Bobby. Pretty much everything I can say about him I shared in *Unshackled*. I do occasionally see his wife, Arlene, and daughter, Chrissy—most recently at my sister Mary's funeral. I'm grateful they came and endeavor to stay in touch.

I have heard more recently of Sid. His attorney today, who ironically was the Assistant District Attorney during my release in 2012, is working on having his sentence revisited. I occasionally see members of his family when I'm in Pennsylvania. I hope he will get a chance at freedom. I pray that he will come to find his place in God's story.

Orlando, Hammer, Henry, Raffy, Louie, Raffy, Doc—I love these guys! I can't wait until the next opportunity we all have to get together. I pray it's here at my home in Fort Worth. We can celebrate what God is doing in all our lives

... and when we do, we're going to grab an electric cord and some paper clips and make Darin a chichi!

Thank You for Reading

Thank you for taking the time to read *LIFE After Unshackled.*
I hope you've enjoyed reading my story as much as I've enjoyed sharing it with you.

Gene McGuire

Gene McGuire is an in-demand speaker, sharing his testimony and teaching on matters of faith. For information on scheduling Gene to speak or to order more copies of his books, visit his website **genemcguire.org** or contact him via email at **gene4192@gmail.com** or postal mail:

Gene McGuire
PO Box 163443
Fort Worth, Texas 76161

Connect with Gene on social media:

Darin Michael Shaw

Darin Michael Shaw is an experienced ghost and collaborative writer. His clients include some of the most well-known and respected ministers, ministries, non-profit and humanitarian organizations in the world today.
darinmichaelshaw.com